The African American HomeBuyers Guide®

Homebuying information for us®

By Imani Afryka

AAHBG LLC

Providers of Exceptional Information for Extraordinary People®

Harlem, NY • Bowie, MD • Omaha, NE

African American HomeBuyers Guide®
Published by
AAHBG LLC.
P.O. Box 2714
New York, NY 10027
www.AAHBG.com

Copyright © 2003 Imani Afryka.

All rights reserved. No part of this book, including interior design, cover design, and icons, may be reproduced or transmitted in any form, by any means (electronic, photocopying, recording, or otherwise) without the prior written permission of the publisher.

ISBN: 0974352-0-8

Distributed in the United States by AAHBG LLC

For general information and sales inquiries and special prices on bulk, quantities please visit us at www.AAHBG.com

LIMIT OF LIABILITY/DISCLAIMER OF WARRANTY: THE PUBLISHERS AND AUTHOR HAVE USED THEIR BEST EFFORTS IN PREPARING THIS BOOK. THE PUBLISHER AND AUTHOR MAKE NO REPRESENTATIONS OR WARRANTIES WITH RESPECT TO THE ACCURACY OR COMPLETENESS OF THE CONTENTS AND SPECIFICALLY DISCLAIM ANY IMPLIED WARRANTIES OF MERCHANTABILITY OR FITNESS FOR A PARTICULAR PURPOSE. THERE ARE NO WARRANTIES, WHICH EXTEND BEYOND THE DESCRIPTIONS CONTAINED IN THIS PARAGRAPH. NO WARRANTY MAY BE CREATED OR EXTENDED BY SALES REPRESENTATIVES OR WRITTEN SALES MATERIALS. THE ACCURACY AND COMPLETENESS OF THE INFORMATION PROVIDED HEREIN AND THE OPINIONS STATED HEREIN ARE NOT GUARANTEED OR WARRANTED TO PRODUCE ANY PARTICULAR RESULTS, AND THE ADVICE AND STRATEGIES CONTAINED HEREIN MAY NOT BE SUITABLE FOR EVERY INDIVIDUAL. NEITHER THE PUBLISHER NOR AUTHOR SHALL BE LIABLE FOR ANY LOSS OF PROFIT OR ANY OTHER COMMERCIAL DAMAGES, INCLUDING BUT NOT LIMITED TO SPECIAL, INCIDENTAL, CONSEQUENTIAL, OR OTHER DAMAGES.

Dedications

This guide is dedicated to the African American homebuyers and homeowners who shared their joys and sorrows. We are building a peaceful world one homeowner at a time.

To my father Milton McKay King Polk: he gave us a home when we didn't have a house.

To my spiritual grandfather Daisaku Ikeda whose courage, compassion, joy and faith has determined my life.

Author's Acknowledgments

The incredible effort it took to publish this book for our people was made possible by the following. My mom Donna Polk Primm from whom I am twice born, thank you for giving me life, then allowing me to enjoy it by introducing me to the SGI and Buddhism. My brother Mark who financed the entire project and will have his book finished right after law school. My brother Marlon, your work ethic is unbelievable and still you find time to spend time with the kids, thanks also for making your law firm available for which I give thanks to Kathy and Margo. My brother Marcus, I love you as you love me. Joanie thanks for the legal advice and the poetry. Gratitude to my extended family of in-laws, nieces and nephews and to my grandparents, Mays, Polks, Kings and Gadlings, I honor and seek you out.

Thanks to Dahlia P. without you this book would only be four pages of pictures. Edwin M. for 13 years of friendship and counting. The crew: Molly, Hosea J and Lil Dahlia L, Mandy and Delores for giving me your time. Alan Young for advice, Donna Walker Kuhne for your extraordinary wisdom and joy. Queen Afua for transforming my health consciousness. Attorney Alton Maddox and the UAM for educating our people. Terrie Williams for that long ago writing assignment. Much love to my SGI family and especially to Harlem's Apollo District. Cyrille and staff at MNN.

The Staff at Carver Bank especially Sheryl Glover and Deborah Wright, Gloria Dulan-Wilson, Jersey City Housing Coordinator, Janice Stewart of the Atlanta Housing Authority, Leon Gelzer, Northeast Brooklyn Housing Dev Corp, NACA, The Crew at Bowne. The Rothschild Team. The staff at FannieMae and FreddieMac. The Schomburg Library for having all the statistics and stories on black people that anyone ever needed.

If you should find errors in this wonderful book it is solely due to the author's adamant persistence that won over the wise objections of one of the English language's best editors, Dr. Ross Primm. Thank you.

Kimani & Kanika
My beautiful sisters
and brother
Please live a harmonious
and peaceful life
and keep a home

Imani

Table of Contents

PREFACE **3**

INTRODUCTION **7**
   Commitments To Becoming A Homeowner 8
   Challenges Towards Homeownership 11

CHAPTER 1
The Good And The Oh Yes, Of Homeownership **17**
   Advantages Of Homeownership 17
   Responsibilities of Homeownership 20
   Single Owner or Co-Owners (Dealing with Drama) 21
   In or Out of the Vail – Black or Non-Black Neighborhoods 24
   Dream Homes for Real People 25

CHAPTER 2
Making The Dream A Reality **29**
   Getting Organized 30
   Introducing Your Home Dream Team 34

CHAPTER 3
Show Me The Money **53**
   Getting Pre-qualified vs. Pre-approved 54
   The Costs Of Purchasing A House 55
   10 Credit Scams That Affect African Americans 67
   Increasing Your Borrowing Power 76
   Correcting Your Credit, The Help You Need 80

CHAPTER 4
A House Is Not A Home, Until You Buy It **87**
   Is There A Home For Me? 88
   Negotiating The Home Purchase 93

CHAPTER 5
Buying Your Mortgage **101**
   Shopping for a mortgage 102
   Applying for a loan 112
   What to do if your loan is denied 118

CHAPTER 6
Finally, It's My House Now — 123
What to Do Before the "Closing" 124
"Closing Day" 130
Buyer's Remorse (I Paid How Much?) 1333

CHAPTER 7
Homeowning, Like You Love It — 135
Home and Happy 137
Avoiding Foreclosure Like the Plague 143
Refinancing 158

APPENDIXES
Resources — 161
Organizations That Help You Buy a Home 161
Downpayment Assistance 165
How Much Money Is It – Finder 169
Pre-Application Information Worksheet 171
Budget Worksheet 173
Mortgage Shopping Comparison Worksheet 174
Top Ten Black Cities For Living and Working* 175

GLOSSARY — 176

INDEX — 186

BIBLIOGRAPHY — 191

Preface

"It takes a village to raise a child"

—African Proverb

"It takes love and commitment to raise a village"

—Imani Afryka

So, you want to be a homeowner. Wonderful! Fantastic! You may have heard on T.V., and radio or read in the newspapers, that interest rates are at their lowest point in many years. You may have also heard that homes in the community are going fast and that prices are skyrocketing. You are sure you heard that owning a home would save you more money than renting. Currently, interest rates are at their lowest in forty years, so this is the time to consider becoming a homeowner. Home prices have risen around the country, but there are affordable homes for you in today's market. Being a homeowner is the surest means to accumulating wealth in America. Becoming a homeowner is one of the most positive actions you can take for improving the financial and social condition for yourself and your family as well.

Sounds great, but what do you do now to become a homeowner? There are other messages that you may have heard. Messages such as; lenders don't lend money to African Americans to buy homes, (which isn't true). Or, if lenders are lending money, they are charging African Americans higher interest rates or hidden fees, (which is sometimes true). Or if everything is fair on the lenders side, you still don't know how to go about buying a home in a way that will save you money and aggravation (too true!). No problem. The answer to avoiding all of the negative effects and receiving the positive benefits of being a homeowner is within the African American HomeBuyers Guide. The information in this book is the collected wisdom and experience of real estate professionals; real estate agents, brokers, mortgage bankers, lenders, inspectors combined together to help you learn and understand the home buying process. Listening to homebuyers and homeowners just like you and providing easy to understand answers to their questions was the goal in writing this guide. Your buying a home in today's market will prove that the goal was accomplished.

The challenge in learning home buying techniques is learning to believe in yourself and believing that you can be a successful homeowner. Janice Stewart of the Atlanta Housing Authority, who has assisted hundreds of families in buying their first homes, mentioned that her most difficult struggle is convincing people to stay focused on their goal and to not give up when the process becomes challenging. Janice says, "You need to have a strong desire to own a home, it is also important that you do not give up when everything seems hopeless. You can own a home if you are determined."

This guide is written with the understanding that many people buy homes together as married or non-married couples, mother and daughter, and in some cases, friends looking to share the cost of homeownership. It was also written for the single buyer as well. Home buying patterns are changing and single women are the fastest growing segment of homeowners in the African American community. Endowed with amazing persistence and faith, black women are overcoming the double barrier of sexism and racism to establish homes for themselves and their children. These women are not waiting for Mr. Right or even Mr. Right Now to buy homes, and neither should you if you are a single black queen. Of course, anyone and everyone, whether single or married, can benefit from the information in this guide.

Feel free to read the whole guide from beginning to end, mastering the entire home buying process, or read only the chapters that apply to your immediate situation.

The need for the African American HomeBuyers Guide

When asked "With all of the home buying books available today. Why did you write the African American HomeBuyers Guide?" I answer simply, "We needed a book for ourselves." After reading the leading home buying books on the market, I realized few if any of those books addressed the challenges and situations faced by African Americans going through the home buying process. Although there are millions of African Americans (Caribbean Americans, Africans and Hispanics included) who are buying homes right now and building wonderful communities, nevertheless there are millions more, who are shut out of the home buying market. The lack of useful information and shortage of resources for our people to buy a home is astonishing. According to the 2000 Census, there are currently around 6.3 million African American homeowners (48% of all households) , and 7.0 million African American renters (53%). This is almost the complete opposite of white Americans, who are listed at (74%) homeowners and (25%) renters. Even with the low numbers of homeowners, African Americans are leading the country in foreclosures, unethically high interest rates, and declined loans. The primary reason for these negative statistics, of course, is the enduring legacy of racism and discrimination. In February of 2003, Angelo R. Mozilo, Chairman of Countrywide, the largest mortgage bank in America, spoke at a national housing industry meeting in Washington D.C., stating, "Although it may not be the issue it once was, discrimination still exists. And make no mistake – it has an impact on the homeownership rate of minority families."

Discrimination is not the only issue keeping more African Americans from becoming homeowners. A secondary and just as powerful reason is the lack of education and information on the part of African Americans regarding the home buying process, thus, the need for a guide written solely for us.

The contents of each chapter are as follows:

Chapter 1: The Good And The Oh Yes, Of Homeownership. We will take a realistic look at the benefits and responsibilities of owning a home. This chapter will include costs and types of neighborhoods and homes available.

Chapter 2: Making The Dream Home A Reality. We will focus on getting organized and introducing you to the people who will help you buy your home, such as a real estate agent, mortgage broker, and your support person.

Chapter 3: Show Me The Money. This chapter offers a clear method to understanding how much money you will need to buy a home. You will also determine how much money you have available right now for a down payment. Included is an in-depth credit repair section, providing clear steps for you to deal with your credit.

Chapter 4: A House Is Not A Home, Until You Buy It. With the limited number of homes available to African Americans living near urban centers, knowing where and how to find and purchase a home is vital and is the focus of this chapter. We will also discuss negotiating tips and the importance of inspecting a home.

Chapter 5: **Buying Your Mortgage**. We discuss the details of shopping for a mortgage and what to look for in a lender. You will also have a clearer understanding on how a lender determines if you will get a loan. There is also a valuable section on protecting yourself from destructive predatory lending.

Chapter 6: Finally, It's My House Now. This chapter covers what will happen at the closing process (the event where you become the owner of the house) and the steps you must take before closing. We will ease your anxiety regarding the "Closing" by explaining what you are responsible for and the documents you will be required to sign.

Chapter 7: Homeowning, Like You Love It. This chapter provides a positive glimpse of life as a homeowner. We also cover the importance of paying your mortgage on time and explain what you can do if you ever run into financial problems.

Appendix: We conclude with the information everyone really wants. The organizations that provide you with the help you need to buy a home (mucho cash, in some cases). I added several forms and worksheets to help you complete the loan application process.

Glossary of real estate terms and an index and bibliography of the books and some of the sources used in writing this guide.

Thank you for buying the *African American HomeBuyers Guide*.

Introduction

"I come here celebrating every African, every colored, black Negro American everywhere that ever cooked a meal, ever raised a child, ever worked in the fields, ever went to school, ever sang in a choir, ever loved a man or loved a woman, every corn-rowed, every Afroed, every wig-wearing, pigtailed, weave-wearing one of us. I come celebrating the journey. I come celebrating the little passage, the movement of our women people."

–Oprah Winfrey, 1954 – , Entertainer

"Every [black] family shall have a plot of not more than forty acres of tillable ground."

–William T. Sherman, 1820-1891, U.S. General Special Field Orders, Savannah, GA, Jan 16, 1865

Welcome, and congratulations on beginning your homebuyer's journey. Whether you are a single parent, a married couple, a mother and daughter, or whether you earn $20,000 or more than $200,000 the *African American HomeBuyers Guide* was written to support you in your effort to becoming a homeowner. The information and advice within this book will help you succeed in becoming a smart homeowner. You will understand the entire home buying process that African Americans encounter when dealing with the real estate and financing industry.

For many African Americans owning a home is seen as a rite-of-passage. Homeownership symbolizes that a person has achieved a certain economic status and demonstrated the virtues necessary to prosper in a sometimes hostile environment. Nevertheless, only 48% of African Americans own their homes compared to 54% Asian Americans homeowners and 74% of Caucasian Americans. Clearly, more African Americans can and need to make this rite-of-passage.

Commitments To Becoming A Homeowner

Your Commitment

Becoming a homeowner is possible for you regardless of the many obstacles that you may encounter. Like many African Americans, you might be concerned about your credit card debt, a shaky job situation, relationship drama or many other challenges. You should be concerned about those issues, they are very important. Nevertheless, even with those issues, you have to live somewhere. Don't hesitate, start now on the path to becoming a homeowner. Committing yourself completely in mind, body and spirit to becoming a homeowner will begin activating powerful good forces in your life. These forces, which I will call the AAHBG Angels come in many forms, money arriving when you most need it, tips on housing programs from complete strangers, or pens that never leave ink on your clothes, when filling out loan applications. Good positive forces occur when you commit yourself to this worthwhile endeavor. Self-confidence and a positive attitude will help you immensely in your effort, so affirmations are included to support your home buying determination. In time, each aspect of your life will move towards a more financially healthy, balanced and joyful home environment.

Federal Government's Commitment

A commitment to help you become a homeowner is also coming from the federal government. For generations, the federal government participated in preventing African Americans from owning property by creating laws making it illegal for us to do so. The struggles of courageous African Americans significantly; Dr. Martin Luther King, A. Phillip Randolph, Fannie Lou Hamer and many others who are not as well known, including Native Americans, other peoples of color and white Americans influenced our government to do the right thing. The federal government passed the Fair Housing Act in April 1968. This act passed immediately after the assassination of Dr. King, led to the creation of the Department of Housing and Urban Development (HUD), and the passing of the Title VIII of the Civil Rights Act. Title VIII, included the prohibition of discrimination in the sale, rental, and financing of dwellings, and in other housing-related transactions, based on race, color, national origin, religion, sex, and familial status.

The passing of fair housing legislation and creation of organizations such as HUD, has directly led to the increase of African Americans who own their homes today. More resources and monies are owed to African Americans for the many injustices done them. Generations of doing right cannot possibly correct problems that over 400 years of doing wrong has created, but this is a start, and we must make use of it. HUD is a useful organization and has resources and programs available to homebuyers, lenders, and other housing related organizations to increase the level of homeownership in the African American community. Use the resources provided by HUD to your advantage, you will be helping the people at HUD fulfill their mission, of providing housing for all Americans.

The President's Commitment

In June 2002, President Bush issued several proposals to add an additional 5 million African American and people of color homeowners by the end of the decade. Citing that it would be good for America and good for business, President Bush proposed programs such as the American Dream Downpayment Fund. A $200 million program designed to assist qualified homebuyers with their down payment costs. The President also is proposing a Single-Family Affordable Housing Tax Credit, that will provide approximately $2.4 billion to encourage the production of 200,000 affordable homes for sale to low and moderate-income families, and a new "Section 8", homeownership pilot program, that contributes a portion of government subsidized rent payment, towards the down payment on a home. It will be up to us to utilize these programs should they become widely available.

The President also called on the real estate and finance industries to do their part in increasing the level of black homeowners by offering the "America's Homeownership Challenge." This challenge was issued to the real estate and finance industries to make lending and other home buying services available on a wider basis to support the increase in the number of African American homeowners.

Financial and Real Estate Industry's Commitment

Fannie Mae, the largest provider of mortgage financing in the country, has answered the call. Under the leadership of Franklin Raines, Fannie Mae in its American Dream Commitment has pledged to contribute at least $420 billion in mortgage investments to primary lenders to serve more than five million minority households in this decade.

Commercial banks and major mortgage companies are hiring more African American mortgage loan officers, leading to the increase of loans being made to the African American community.

Traditionally, a homebuyer would be expected to make a 20% down payment or 5-10% in a government program. Banks, such as black owned and operated Carver Federal in New York, have made mortgage products that require as little as 3% down payment available. Many other black financial institutions are responding with creative community based programs geared to fund home buying.

Real estate companies are recognizing the need to better serve the African American community. These agencies are seeking black real estate brokers and educating their existing staff on the needs and sensitivity of African American homebuyers.

On a local level, organizations such as the Greater Harlem Real Estate Board, led by Mr. Orlando Rivera, have been offering homeownership seminars and other services directly to prospective homebuyers. NACA (naca.com) and ACORN (acorn.org) are both national organizations that work directly with underserved homebuyers providing much needed services and advocacy on behalf of low and moderate income homeowners. Search the yellow pages and the internet for organizations such as these in your areas.

African American Organization's Commitment

Contributing through various educational and legal programs, the NAACP and the National Urban League through its local offices nationwide are constantly affirming their commitment to African American homeownership by sponsoring programs in assistance with Fannie Mae and other organizations.

Publications such as *Black Enterprise*, *Ebony* and *Essence* are providing needed information on a monthly basis that focuses on finances as well as home buying issues.

Religious and Spiritual Community's Commitment

The Black Church has been committed to the building of strong families and the achievement of community development since its inception. As the largest and most powerful organization for African Americans in the world, it has an opportunity to continue setting the direction for the black community by leading in the planning and enacting of programs that will provide housing, financing and other resources for the black home buying community. Other religious and spiritual organizations should also increase their support of housing education and ownership programs.

Challenges Towards Homeownership

It is significant that none of the many home buying books available from mainstream publishers discuss the negative experiences faced by African Americans and people of color. These books, written mainly by white authors for mainly white Americans, do not mention the struggle with redlining, and other forms of discrimination that most Africans Americans have to deal with when planning to buy a home. Many of the leading home buying books do contain information that is useful or at least I found them to be so. Authors Ray Brown and Robert Irwin know more about home owning than almost anyone in the country, white or black. I do recommend using their books when necessary. Increasing your information base is important. Nevertheless, you should be critical if you find information that doesn't reflect or celebrate your perspective, filter it carefully.

African Americans have had little alternative in home buying information by which to educate ourselves. This situation has led us to accept what we're told by lenders, real estate agents and other people in the real estate industry, who at times have not had our best interests in mind. It should come as no surprise that more African Americans rent their homes today than own. The home buying process was not designed for us, and was in some cases designed against us. Now is the time to correct this situation.

A major strength that African Americans possess is our deep faith and perseverance in overcoming difficult situations. Another strength is our ability to stand together to support each other. This guide will support these strengths with education and information to transform the home buying obstacles we encounter into home owning opportunities.

Disarming Racism with Success-ism

It will take more than information and education for African Americans to successfully endure the rigors of the home buying process and possibly face disrespectful and intimidating situations. We must first believe that we can become homeowners, and this requires dealing with our attitude and the reality of living in a racist society.

In *Black Folks Guide to Making Big Money in America*, George Trower-Subira breaks down the issue of attitude and racism in an interesting and clever manner. I reprint this at length because I believe it sets a clear picture of where we are and what attitude we must adopt in order to be successful, not only in homeownership, but in many areas of our life.

The conditions that hold Black folks in poverty are both internal and external in nature…I will define internal as being those factors over which you have substantial control. These factors would include your education, your energy, creative ability, contacts, job skills, choice of mate, number of children, etc.

The external factors are those over which you have very little or no control and would include racism, the interest rates, natural disasters, etc. Of all the factors and variables that have been at work on Black folks in the last say 100 years influencing our ability to survive or perish, one has stood out among the rest: racism. Racism is continuous and unyielding. Black folks can eventually adjust to the price of oil, natural disaster, fire and the loss of a job. But racism is like a shadow following you constantly everywhere you go, or so it seems. I think it is beneficial in this volume to look at reality straight in the eye and realize the following:

a. Racism (the belief of Whites that they are better, more intelligent or more deserving of some privilege or opportunity for no other reason than the fact that they are White) is a reality in all White folks for one reason or another and to some degree or another. But racism doesn't stop all White folks from working in partnership with non-Whites (Blacks included) when there is a buck to be made. This is proven every day.

b. Racism has been used by many of us Blacks as an excuse for lack of determination in pursuing our goal simply because it was a pain in the ass and dampened our spirits. Every single successful Black person in the history of this country, whether they were rich or not, had to overcome racism. It is probably less of an excuse for failing now, for the strong and the determined, than ever before in the history of this racist nation.

c. You can control, if you decide to, so many factors in your life and you can learn to analyze so many situations in your life that you can actually force White folks (at least the ones you "need" and the ones who "need" you) to change the way that they respond to you and "get over." … But when you understand, how Muhammad Ali, …and Dr. Martin Luther King "forced" White folks to change the way they responded and reacted to them then you understand what I mean by overcoming racism. I do not mean that you must be a "great" man or woman to change the face of racism. But once you are serious about yourself and your goals, say what you mean and mean what you say, and force all parties to respect you and what you stand for, you will find certain White folks ready to do business. They may be racist, but most of them [ain't] crazy.

I will not dwell too much more on racism [in this book] because I believe that positive-minded persons should concentrate on doing all the correct and positive things and the negative things, like racism, will be much less of a factor. Action on your part, not my discussion in this book, will expose the shortcomings of the so-called all-powerful deterrent of racism.

The factors holding Black folks in poverty are for the most part not racially identifiable. Most of the things that hold us in poverty are the same things that hold poor White folks in poverty. The faster individuals from either group overcome their drawbacks, the faster they'll close in on the pot of gold.

Mr. Subira has strong opinions, many of which I believe will help you become better equipped to accomplish your goals. No matter what your situation, you can buy and keep a home. Make a strong determination and create a vision of your success in your heart and mind. With over 6 million homeowners of African heritage and more coming everyday, we are becoming homeowners at a rate that was beyond the comprehension of our fore-parents a few generations ago.

Of course, there are some examples in the younger generation, of people winning over racism through success-ism. Tiger Woods, Serena, and Venus Williams are excellent examples. Their amazing success has come through perseverance and deep faith. The commitment they made to become the best spurred them to continue improving and learning their craft when no-one knew who they were. The faith on the part of their parents, who believed in them before anyone else, became their own faith that they could become successful. Working extraordinarily hard has made them excellent and the best at what they do. It has made them Champions. This commitment to excellence has forced white people to adjust to them and has reduced the influence that racism has over their ability to accomplish their goals. By winning consistently, Tiger Woods and the Williams sisters have changed the face of golf and tennis. These champions are a few of the many African Americans we can use as role models of winning over racism with success-ism. Many successful people who have won over the influence of racism are all around you. They may not be famous, yet they are beautiful, powerful and victorious just the same, and they may be looking for someone to encourage. So, keep your eyes, ears and hearts open to their call.

To become a successful homeowner you will need a plan, information, persistence, and courage. The plan and information are provided in this book. The persistence and courage you were given at birth, let it come forth. In one of my favorite books, *The Human Revolution*, Daisaku Ikeda, writes, "a great human revolution in just a single individual will help achieve a change in the destiny of a nation, and further, will enable a change in the destiny of all mankind." All you have to do is become a homeowner.

The AAHBG home buying plan to homeownership

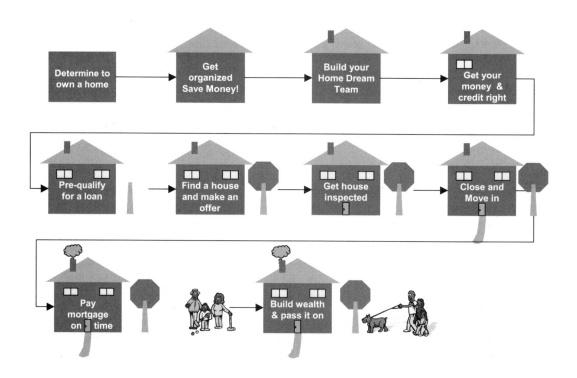

The following guidelines were suggested by homebuyers and homeowners that I have met. We combined them into the African American HomeBuyers Guides to Success. Abide by these guidelines and you will remain on course to achieving your home buying goals.

The African American HomeBuyers Guides to Success

1. Believe in my power and be powerful in my belief.

2. I will educate myself to the best of my ability.

3. If I can't afford it, I won't buy it, because I will lose it.

4. When I find the perfect home, I will buy it immediately.

5. I will read the fine print, or it will cost me!

6. When it isn't in writing, it will cost me!

7. When I don't understand what the writing means, it will cost me!

8. I will keep a written record of everything I agree to and pay for, or it will cost me!

9. I will be patient, persistent, and double check everything, or it will cost me!

10. I am greater than all obstacles I will face – that's already been paid for by the ancestors!

I trust that you will use the information within to achieve your goal of buying the most excellent home available and establishing a wonderful life within it.

Affirmation

I am completely responsible for my decisions, and I choose to be positive and joyful.

Chapter 1
THE GOOD AND THE OH YES, OF HOMEOWNERSHIP

"The lack of wealth to buy a home creates a vicious cycle, because owning a home is the single, most common and powerful way to build wealth in America."

–Franklin D. Raines – Chairman and CEO, Fannie Mae

Denise, a beautiful mother of three teenage children, shares her experience of buying a home. "The thought of buying a home was overwhelming. The anxiety I felt going through the loan qualification process was compounded by the fact that I was going through a painful divorce, with my husband of 16 years. I had to find a home for my kids, my mother and myself." After seven months of searching, Denise finally found a home and closed three months later. "Oh Yes! I found the perfect place, a 1 ½ family home. It's perfect! It has a bedroom for each of the kids, and mother lives in her own full-size apartment downstairs and the children are still near to their father." Denise was amazed at the feelings of pride and confidence she felt when she finally took the keys and moved in. Denise says, "I was standing at the door of my home, my home! I wanted to jump up and down screaming, laughing, crying. I did it. I bought a house on my own. I felt that if I could buy this home, I could do anything."

Where We're Going In This Chapter

You should start the home-buying process by taking a realistic look at what you can expect from homeownership – the rewards as well as the increased responsibilities and the costs involved. If you are sure you are ready, then proceed with confidence, if not—then proceed with confidence and caution.

Advantages Of Homeownership

When you buy a home, you will experience a sense of pride that is at times unbelievable. It will be impossible to walk with a straighter back or your head higher than after buying your first home. Your friends and family will be impressed, and the entire community will look upon you with awe. When you finally turn the key and open the door to your new home, you will feel years younger. This may be overstating things a bit, but the benefits of being a homeowner sometimes seem this fantastic. Nevertheless, there are many real and lasting benefits and responsibilities to being a homeowner, such as the following:

Stability and Well-being

Homeowners experience a sense of well being knowing that they have permanency. A permanent home can increase your emotional as well as physical stability. Homeownership can stabilize property values, which affects the quality of the schools, which has a long-term impact on dropout rates and related crime rates. Furthermore, having control over your living situation reduces the sense of anxiety that comes with not knowing what a landlord might decide to do with your apartment. You have the opportunity to create a healthy and peaceful environment for your family.

Children of Homeowners

A Joint Center for Housing Studies of Harvard University, study *Impact of Homeownership on Child Outcomes* by Haurin, Parcel and Haurin, suggest that children of homeowners have better home environments, high cognitive test scores, and fewer behavior problems than do children of renters. They found that these results hold even after controlling for a large number of economic, social, and demographic variables. Owning a home compared with renting leads to a 13 - 23 percent higher quality of living environment for the children of homeowners. On average, children of homeowners achieve math scores up to nine percent higher, reading scores up to seven percent higher, and reductions in children's behavior problems of up to three percent.

Community Status

First-time homeowners often find that buying a home brings with it enhanced status and a sense of belonging in the neighborhood and the community. You may find that property ownership also brings with it the perception that you are a responsible, tax-paying adult who can contribute to the local economy and who deserves a voice in local government, a perception that is often true.

Strengthening Black Communities

If you are among the many who are buying homes in the revitalized black urban centers, you will be able to share in the pride of laying the foundation for a renaissance in the black community. The Harlem Renaissance, in the early part of the 20th century was also supported by the establishment of a small but devoted number of black homeowners and business people who made a commitment to caring for their neighborhoods, as well as the artists who brought recognition to the community.

The benefits of living in a black community are often overlooked in the discussion of integration. Benefits such as shared cultural values and family support. A sense of pride and the desire to preserve and strengthen black institutions is another motivator for many African Americans to remain in black communities. Although many black neighborhoods are described in negative terms, many are strong and vibrant. African American communities such as Bowie and Mitchellville in Maryland, and Chatham in Chicago, Illinois are some of the most affluent and beautiful neighborhoods in the nation.

Financial Incentives

Homeownership also offers significant financial benefits, such as the following:

Stable housing costs. Rental housing costs typically increase from year to year. If you purchase a home with a fixed-rate mortgage, your monthly mortgage principal and interest payments will remain the same for as long as you own your home. [Insurance cost and taxes do change over the course of the loan] You can also look forward to the day when your mortgage loan is completely paid off.

Tax benefits. The federal government promotes homeownership by providing homeowners with significant tax benefits that are not available to renters. Homeowners can deduct the interest they pay on their mortgage, as well as the property taxes paid to a state or local jurisdiction. When selling, homeowners also benefit from capital gains tax exclusion. These advantages are discussed in more detail in Chapter 7.

Equity investment. Owning a home is also an investment. As you pay down your mortgage, you build up equity (your ownership interest) in your home. Monthly mortgage payments can be seen as a type of scheduled savings plan. Not only are you putting money into property that will likely appreciate (become more valuable over time), you are also buying something that you can borrow against. Again, see Chapter 7. You can sell or pass on to your children or other family members a valuable asset when you are gone, and that they will eventually own outright.

Responsibilities of Homeownership

You should understand that buying a home is a complex, time-consuming and costly process that brings with it sometimes unwelcome responsibilities. You should be prepared to encounter disappointments, delays, and setbacks along the way. Extensive paperwork is involved in any home purchase, much of it difficult to understand without the assistance of an expert.

Considerable time may elapse from the time you decide to purchase a home until the moment you finally unlock your own front door. The process of finding a house and getting financing typically takes several months, especially for the first-time homebuyer. Since most African Americans are concentrated in urban areas where the amount of reasonably priced housing is in short supply the process can take even longer.

Receiving Government Assistance

If you receive public assistance, you need to determine how homeownership will affect your eligibility; you risk losing your benefits if you fail to understand the rules relating to the specific type of assistance you receive. Until recently, for example, according to the U.S. Department of Housing and Urban Development (HUD) "Section 8", vouchers and certificates could be used only to assist in paying rent and could not be applied toward a mortgage payment.

Recipients of Supplemental Security Income (SSI) benefits may not accumulate more than $2,000 in cash resources, while Medicaid recipients may face even more stringent resource limitations, depending on the state in which they live. These restrictions make it difficult to save enough money for a typical down payment and closing costs. Although these obstacles can be overcome, they cannot be ignored.

High Cost of Homeownership

Although owning a home may result in lower living costs over the long term, homeownership usually means an initial increase in housing costs. Even if the mortgage payments do not exceed the rent you are now paying, you will face additional expenses such as routine maintenance and emergency repairs, property taxes, homeowner's and mortgage insurance, and utility payments.

Maintenance and Upkeep

As a homeowner, you will be responsible for maintaining your house (mowing the lawn, shoveling snow, painting the exterior walls) and keeping it in good repair. No longer will you be able to simply call the landlord when something needs to be fixed. One reason for the popularity of condominiums is that condo owners can enjoy owning a home without having complete responsibility for its upkeep.

Decreased Mobility

Homeowners, unlike renters, cannot simply give the landlord notice and move at the end of the month. Selling a house (like buying a house) is a time-consuming endeavor. If you are unsure whether you want to live in the same place for more than a year or two, this might not be the ideal time to buy a house. You may wish to explore a number of neighborhoods, towns, or even different areas of the country before making a decision to purchase a home.

Possibility of Foreclosure

If you fail to pay your monthly mortgage payments on time, the bank or other lender can (and will) foreclose on the property. The lender will sell the house in an attempt to recover the money it loaned. This can result not only in the loss of your home (and all the money you have paid on the mortgage to date), but it will also have a long-term, adverse impact on your credit rating. It's critical that you are certain you can afford the home you choose to buy.

Sharing the Cost of Homeownership

One path to buying a home when your individual financial situation is not strong is to pool your resources with another homebuyer. The combining of financial and other resources is characteristic of African, Asian, and Indian peoples. "Pooling your money with other responsible people can get you into a home and allow you to begin accumulating equity and other financial benefits much sooner than going it alone." says Gloria Dulan-Wilson, Housing Coordinator for Jersey City, New Jersey.

Single Owner or Co-Owners (Dealing with Drama)

The title is the document that states who is the legal owner of a property. When two or more people co-own a property, the number of ways to take title multiplies dramatically.

How title is held is critically important. Each form of co-ownership has its own rainbow of advantages, disadvantages, tax consequences, and legal repercussions. You shouldn't make this decision in haste at an escrow office while signing your closing papers. Unfortunately, that's what usually happens and it can and often leads to emotional, mental, and legal drama.

Before you arrive at a decision similar to that just mentioned, have a lawyer draft an agreement between you and any other co-owners. No matter how much you're in-love now, or how long you have been best friends, get ownership details in legally binding writing. What should you include in your written agreement. The following are good provisions:

- Provisions to buy out a co-owner who has to sell when the other owner wants to keep the property;

- Provisions to prorate maintenance and repair costs among co-owners with unequal shares in the property;

- Provisions to resolve disputes regarding such things as what color to paint the house;

- Provisions for penalties for a co-owner who can't cover his or her share of loan payments or property taxes;

These provisions are just for starters. Many other details need to be considered in taking title that can't be covered in this book. It is important that you find a competent real estate lawyer to answer any questions you may have in this area.

What's the best form of co-ownership for you? That depends on your circumstances. Here are some forms of co-ownership and the advantages of each type:

Joint Tenancy

If you and your mother want to buy a house together, you would sign documents as joint tenants. The main characteristic of joint tenancy is that the surviving joint tenant takes the property (whether the property is real estate, a bank account, a stock, a bond or mutual fund account) upon the death of the other joint owner regardless of what the Will or other estate plan of the deceased person may provide. This may not be the intent of the original joint tenants because it bars descendants, heirs, or beneficiaries other than the other surviving joint tenants from receiving any interest in the property. This feature of joint tenancy co-ownership is known as the right of survivorship.

Married couples, and soon-to-be-married couples are the primary parties that utilize this form of taking title. Less often, but still possible, joint tenancy relationships are mother-daughter situations and other two party agreements. Unfortunately, joint tenancy is not as simple or clear as most people think. Joint tenancy may have other consequences. For example, if property of any kind is put into a joint tenancy with a relative who receives public assistance or other benefits such as social security disability, the relative's entitlement to these benefits may be jeopardized. Further, the creditors of the joint tenant may seek to collect a debt from the property or from the proceeds resulting from a forced judicial sale of the property. Other aspects of a joint tenancy, which should be considered, are that all joint tenants must agree to the sale of real estate.

Community Property

Only married couples can take title as community property. An advantage of community property co-ownership is the ability to will your share of the house to whomever you wish. Due to the right of survivorship, this choice isn't possible when title is held as joint tenants. An advantage of community property co-ownership is that both halves of your house get a stepped-up basis upon the death of your spouse. This gives you a big tax savings.

Here's how a stepped-up basis works. Say, for example, that you and your spouse paid $180,000 for the house when you bought it. Immediately after your spouse's death, the house is appraised at $300,000.

Your new cost-of-the-home basis for tax purposes is now $300,000. Capital gains tax is forgiven on every penny of appreciation in value between the date of purchase and the time your spouse died.

Tenants-in-common or Partnerships

Holding title as tenants-in-common or in the form of a partnership doesn't entitle the tax advantages of a stepped-up basis upon the death of a co-owner. Nevertheless, offsetting legal advantages do exist, for unrelated persons who take title either as tenants-in-common or as a partnership. Under these forms of co-ownership, you generally have the right to will or sell your share of the property without permission of the co-owners. Furthermore, co-owners don't have to have equal ownership interests in the property. This is perfect when someone is helping you buy a property but isn't willing or able to put down a large amount.

Now you have an understanding of how to take title, take the time to discuss it openly and as honestly as possible with your potential co-owner and agree to get everything in writing before you get to the closing table.

In or Out of the Vail – Black or Non-Black Neighborhoods

Statistically, the majority of African Americans live in or near urban areas in predominately black communities. Nevertheless, more African Americans have moved into the suburbs of cities such as Houston, Atlanta, Detroit, Los Angeles and Philadelphia, these communities are also predominately Black. Some African Americans have made a choice to move into mixed ethnic and or white neighborhoods. There are benefits to be found where ever you chose to live. Be sure to carefully weigh what is important to you when looking at a neighborhood. Maintain flexibility, perseverance, and diligence. This may be the first time you have had a choice about where you live. The following questions may be helpful as you attempt to characterize your ideal neighborhood:

- Would you like to find a house in the area in which you currently live? Is there family or friends you would like to live close to?

- Are there better opportunities for finding a job or childcare in some neighborhoods than in others?

- Does the thought of dealing with overt racism deter you from feeling comfortable in certain neighborhoods?

- Is it important that your neighbors reflect your cultural heritage?

- Do you rely on public transportation? If so, is it available and convenient for you to use?

- Are you interested in having a pet? A garden? A swimming pool? A nearby park? A video store or grocery store within walking distance?

- Do you enjoy the hustle and bustle of a busy neighborhood with lots of children, or do you prefer a quiet, older community?

- If you will need assistance to live in your new home, does the location affect the availability of such assistance?

- How does the property tax rate compare with other areas? (A real estate agent can help answer this question.)

- How safe is the neighborhood?

- Do you wish to participate in recreational activities, attend a place of worship, or be involved in local politics?

The best way to become familiar with a neighborhood is to spend time exploring it. Take time to wander around and get the feel of different areas until you find a neighborhood that seems right for you. Talk with people you encounter and ask about activities and community services that are available in the area. You should explore the local supermarket, bank, video store, places of worship, and recreation center. What types of medical services are available? Over time, you will be able to narrow the list down to a few of the most desirable neighborhoods.

Dream Homes for Real People

What kind of house do you want to live in? Whether or not you have a vision of your "dream house", you probably have some idea of the type and size of house that suits you. Again, making a wish list may help you assess your house-hunting requirements. What are your needs in terms of style, size, and special features? There are many different styles of home. Again, know what you want but be flexible. A refurbished library can make a great home with the right amount of creativity.

Here are some housing terms that you should understand:

Single-family home. A single-family home is designed to be occupied by one person or household (a family or housemates). It usually stands on its own; although in urban areas, single-family townhouses may share a common wall. The homeowner buys both the house and the lot on which it stands.

Townhouse. Townhomes share common walls and land space with other homes. Townhomes can share the characteristics of several different homes. Not quite the same as condominiums nor are townhomes considered to be single family homes. They can be quite elaborate, but tend to be smaller and less expensive than single-family homes.

Condominium. Condominiums are the "starter home" of choice for many homebuyers today because they are generally smaller and less expensive than single-family houses. The term "condominium" does not describe a particular type of building, but rather a type of joint ownership. Each housing unit is individually owned, while the facilities and common areas (the surrounding land, hallways and elevators, and recreational facilities) are owned collectively by the owners of each unit. In addition to your monthly mortgage payment, condominium owners pay a "condo fee" that pays for management of the complex, upkeep of the common property areas, and sometimes the cost of utilities.

Condominiums combine some of the advantages of apartment living with those of homeownership. Condominium owners reap the same financial benefits (including tax breaks) as other homeowners without many of the traditional chores of homeownership (such as shoveling the walk or hiring a contractor to fix the leaky roof). Many condos offer amenities such as landscaped grounds, meeting rooms, recreation rooms, swimming pools, and play areas for children.

Buying a condominium is more complicated than buying a single-family home. Homebuyers need to investigate not only the specific unit in which they are interested, but also the entire project, from both a physical and a financial standpoint. What do the condo fees cover? What types of expenses must be covered by special assessments, that require additional payments by everyone in the complex? Are there unusual or unexpected expenses (such as street and driveway repaving, exterior painting, or re-roofing) that are not covered by the monthly condo fees?

Cooperative. Cooperatives, or co-ops, are another form of collective ownership. Coop owners buy shares in a corporation that owns the building and land; you do not actually own the individual units you live in. Cooperatives are well established in New York City and in some other parts of the country.

Similar to Condominiums, the owners of Co-ops receive the benefits of shared housing maintenance and upkeep, however the paperwork and legalities for buying a co-op is extensive and complex. Be sure to involve a professional real estate attorney in any transaction involving condo's or co-ops.

Manufactured/Mobile Homes. Manufactured Homes: These are homes built entirely in the factory under a federal building code administered by the U.S. Department of Housing and Urban Development (HUD). Manufactured homes may be single- or multi-section and are transported to the site and installed. The federal standards regulate manufactured housing design and construction, strength and durability, transportability, fire resistance, energy efficiency and quality. The HUD Code also sets performance standards for the heating, plumbing, air-conditioning, thermal, and electrical systems. On-site additions, such as garages, decks and porches, often add to the attractiveness of manufactured homes and must be built to local, state, or regional building codes.

Multi-family homes. This is normally a single structure with several floors. Tenants live in units on each floor and the owner can and usually lives on one or more floors of the building. The owner becomes a landlord and collects rents and maintains the property for himself and the tenants. The cost for these types of homes can be very expensive with the rent offsetting the mortgage price. Some lenders allow the expected rent to be included in the income qualification of the borrower. Because the owner will live in close proximity to his tenants and depends on their rent payments to cover the mortgage, it is essential to locate disciplined tenants. There are laws that determine the responsibilities and rights of the tenants and landlords that an owner must be aware of, to safeguard his or her investment in multi-family homes.

— subletting?

You may not find a house in your price range that offers everything you want, but it helps to be able to tell a real estate agent what features are most important.

Once you have determined what features are most important in a house, you should look again at the neighborhoods you have identified as desirable. What are the neighborhoods that have the kind of houses you want?

You may find the following questions helpful in deciding what sort of house is ideal for you:

- Are you interested in an older home or a brand-new one? Would you prefer to design and build your home?

- Does the idea of a condominium appeal to you? A co-op? A single-family house?

- If you prefer an older home, do you have the resources to make needed repairs and renovations?

- What size house do you require? Be sure to consider your future needs - for example, do you plan to have children or elderly parents to care for?

- How much land would you like to have? Would you like a garden, a play area, space for a pet, a clothesline, or a swimming pool?

- If you choose a home with a large yard, how will you maintain it?

- Is off-street parking important?

- Do you need space for a washer and dryer? A second bathroom? A porch or deck? Is a garage or workshop a necessity?

- Would you like a fireplace? Lots of windows? A hot tub? Air conditioning?

- Do you need a house that is accessible? What is needed to enable you to move about freely?

Chapter 1: The Good And The Oh Yes, Of Homeownership

Where we've been

If you have followed the steps outlined in this chapter, you should be aware of the benefits and responsibilities of homeownership. You can now decide how to take the title of your home and you should have a clearer view of the variety of homes available to you. In the next chapter we will introduce you to the people who will help you buy your home and help you get organized along the way.

Affirmation

I am a reflection of the (Great Creator, Most High, Ultimate Law) and will live my life exuding that awareness.

Chapter 2
MAKING THE DREAM A REALITY

"The time for cynicism is over—and it is you who will help to shape the end of cynicism. It is you—if you will summon the courage—who will forge new initiatives in finance, technology, medicine, and management that will put all Americans back to work and at the same time give America a better shot at feeding the hungry, sheltering the homeless, healing the sick, and caring for the children."

–Myrlie Evers-Williams, NAACP official

"All of us may not live to see the higher accomplishments of an African Empire, so strong and powerful as to compel the respect of mankind, but we, in our lifetime can so work and act as to make the dream a possibility within another generation."

–Marcus Garvey, 1887-1940, Nationalist Leader

Martin was forever late getting to his appointments. Whether it was meeting with a loan officer or seeing a home with his real estate agent, he was not organized and was constantly looking for papers, keys etc. Martin spoke about his difficulty: "I was always misplacing my keys, or cell phone. Whenever it came time to do something important, I wouldn't be able to find a document or the information that I needed." Several years ago, during the negotiation for a $60,000 home, Martin misplaced the number to the real estate agent showing the home. The home sold to someone who responded sooner than Martin. "That's when I knew I had to take control of my life. It took losing a home that is now worth $400,000 for me to learn the value of getting organized," said Martin. After attending an Organizing Your Time and Workplace seminar offered by his company, Martin quickly became the most organized person he knew. Martin adds, "I now own several homes and I keep track of all of my important documents and information in a personal filing system. I don't know how much money being organized has saved me, but I do know I have saved a lot of time, which in the end has been much more valuable."

Where We're Going In This Chapter

In this chapter, you will be introduced to getting organized, collecting your documents, and developing your plan to homeownership. You will also be introduced to some of the people whom you will work with, in the process of buying a home. The people you select to help you buy your home will become part of your Home Dream Team, and just like the Olympic Dream Team's success in basketball, they will help make your home buying process successful.

Getting Organized

There are many ways to accomplish a goal, but being organized will increase your chances of success and reduce your distress by 100%.

Building Your Home-in-a-box

Relax; this is not about actually living in a box. The Home-in-a-box is the box or filing cabinet that will house your documents, loan application, and other information to help your buying process go smoothly. You will also need some basic organizational supplies. Set aside some time to organize your Home-in-a-box filing system. This will make preparing your budget, applying for mortgages, or completing forms much easier. Obtain the best materials you can afford. Display your creative African heritage; build a beautiful and solid Home-in-a-box.

You will need space where you live now for a filing cabinet or box that can hold letter or legal sized paper. This space is your virtual neighborhood, and it is sacred because you will be building your Home-in-a-box there. If you can afford it, consider getting a fireproof safe or investing in a safe deposit box at your local bank. If not, make sure you can at least waterproof your documents.

You can get most of the supplies listed below, from a local office store, or ask for donations from a local business, or bank: experience has shown when people are aware that you are working towards buying a home they are supportive.

You will have to contact various governmental and public institutions to get most of your important documentation. Once you get them, make and keep copies of the documents that would be difficult and expensive to replace.

The following items will help the organizing process:

African American HomeBuyers Guide - If you are borrowing this book, buy one for yourself, as you will probably write and mark in it (and you will be helping to support my efforts in writing more books, and of course, helping me to pay my mortgage.)

Filing cabinet – Any quality filing cabinet or sturdy container that can hold a dozen, letter size file folders and the other items listed below will work.

Dozen letter sized file folders – File folders are crucial to keeping your documents neat and accessible. Spend wisely and get the most durable items for a good price. Don't hesitate to ask for a discount whenever you purchase. Make sure you gather information on each person who will be borrowing money and living in the home.

Label the folders as follows:

Personal – You should have an original of your birth certificate, social security card, educational records, diplomas and GED certificates. Make a copy of your driver's license, state identification card, passport, and medical information. Some of this information will not be used for the home buying process, but you should have it in your possession for emergencies.

Home Dream Team – Keep the names and contact information of every person whom you meet that can help you purchase a home. Business cards, referrals for real estate agents, mortgage brokers, loan officers and a list of people who owe you money go in this folder. When the time comes, they will help you buy your home.

Budget – This folder will hold your monthly and yearly budget information & goals. There is a budget worksheet in the appendix. Complete this as soon as you can and begin saving your money.

Income – Keep a copy of all pay-stubs, alimony payments, child support checks, sou-sou (African & Caribbean name for a rotating credit network) or any other income producing documents you receive. If you work but receive undocumented monies "off the books," find a way to get them into the financial system legally for the amount you wish to claim. Lenders want to see where your money comes from and so does the IRS.

Credit Report – You can get a copy of your credit report for a small fee ranging from around $9.99 to $29.99, or in certain states, you are allowed one free copy each year. Your credit report is probably the single most important document in your files. Lenders measure your willingness and history of repaying your debts by looking at the credit history that is listed in your credit report. There are many different credit reporting agencies but most lenders use these three;

- Equifax (www.equifax.com) Telephone: 1-800-685-1111;
- Experian (www.experian.com) Telephone 1-888-397-3742;
- Trans Union (www.transunion.com) Telephone 1-800-916-8800.

You may also want to get your FICO score at (www.MYFICO.com). Don't panic, credit issues are discussed in detail in Chapter 3.

Loan Information – Keep a file on all bank and lending information you collect. You can keep a completed copy of the loan application template to save time when filling out loan information.

Home Wish List – What does your dream home look like? Describe what you want and do not want in a home. Collect pictures of homes you admire and place them in this folder. When the time comes to look for a home, you will know what you want and what it looks like. You can give this file to your real estate agent to help the agent understand what you are looking for in a home. When you are looking at houses, keep a picture and the details of each home you see in this folder.

Home Maintenance – After purchasing your home, keep copies of blueprints, floor plans, architectural records, historical information, list of contractors and materials suppliers (if you own a newly built home). Keep an audio and or video record of your home and personal belongings for insurance purposes.

Receipts – Begin keeping and organizing all of your receipts. You will notice your spending pattern. Your receipts are also necessary to complete your personal budget. Come tax time it will be easier to locate the information needed to justify your housing deductions.

Employment – Keep copies of hiring letters and employment verification. Keep a list of where you worked, salary, position, supervisor names, and numbers and last day you worked, for each job you had for the past five years.

Financials Information – Collect bank statements for each account you have going back at least the past three months. You need to have the documentation for your tax returns for the past 3 years, 401k statements, or any assets you have, such as stocks, bonds, and jewelry appraisals. Your liabilities such as credit card bills, utilities, and rental payments also can go into this folder.

Home Purchase – Keep track and maintain all of the paperwork that was needed when you applied for your mortgage, in case you refinance. Make sure you keep the deed, mortgage note, settlement statement, title insurance policy, appraisal, disclosures, original comparative market analysis, original real estate listing, and home inspection report in a safe place.

Home Insurance – Place your homeowners, flood, earthquake, or home warranty policies originals in the same safe location as the other important documents and keep the copies in this folder. Also, keep a list of insurance agents or companies and copies of any correspondence related to claims.

Miscellaneous Folder – This folder is for everything else that is left over.

Calculator – To add things up.

Internet Access – Do your best to get access to the Internet. The speed and ease of the Internet is increasing each day. You can find information on just about any topic on the Internet. The price is the same as cable T.V. in most areas, and if you shop around, you can get Internet service combined with your cable or your telephone service. More real estate business is occurring on-line everyday, almost more than in the physical world. Right now, you can do just about everything on the Internet involving your home purchase. You can apply for loans directly on line and find out if you are approved in less than an hour in some cases. If you do not have home or office access, try your public library or local college. If you are not comfortable using a computer, real estate agents, banks and other service providers are still very happy to meet with you in person.

Notebook – Keep notes, telephone numbers, tips and home description in this notebook

A Watch – It is important to always be on time. The number one reason that people are fired from work is lateness. Missing an appointment by even a few seconds can cost you an opportunity to achieve your goals. Successful people arrive to their appointments on time, or even a little early. CP time stands for consistently punctual.

Pens and pencils – Sign your legal documents with blue pens, so you can identify original documents from black and white copies. This is important when you need to know what is an original document.

Stapler, paper clips, letter opener – Use these items to keep you paperwork neat and organized.

A calendar and appointment book – Use both to track what you did and what you need to do on a weekly and monthly basis. Did you send out an application before the deadline? Write it down. What time do you have to meet with your lawyer? Write it down. Keep accurate appointment information such as:

- **Who:** Always get the correct spelling and pronunciation and the name and title of the person you will be meeting.
- **Time:** 3:30 pm – 4:30 pm (include time it will take to get to the appointment on-time)
- **Date:** include the day and date Thursday, February 6, 2003
- **Telephone:** 212 555-1234 (include area code and extensions)
- **Purpose:** Sign contract for home
- **Follow up:** The seller will sign and then contact bank

Your Home-in-a-box is as valuable as the home you will be buying, so keep it organized, locked and secure. There is one last item to include.

Aspirin or herbal equivalent – For the headaches that are sure to come. You can thank me later.

Each week you should set aside a time to do at least one task towards your home buying goal; looking over your budget, adding documentation, or contacting lenders, or checking your debt situation, or attending a home buying seminar.

In the process of organizing and gathering the information for the filing system, you will notice that your life will become more and more organized. You may have to deal with some issues in your life that you have been avoiding. Getting the divorce papers into your personal file may require you to actually complete the divorce procedure. Organizing your files will help you protect the investment you have made and allow you to reap the full benefits of owning your home.

Introducing Your Home Dream Team

In the 1992 Summer Olympics, the world was introduced to America's basketball Dream Team. The Dream Team won game after game against the other teams of the world. Each player was the best at his position. There was Magic Johnson, the floor general, who directed everyone on where to go and what to do, just as you will have to do when working with real estate people.

Then there was Larry Bird, the long distance shooter, who made sure that the other team played fair, and that the other players couldn't gang up on a single team member just as a good real estate attorney will not allow the other parties to take unfair advantage of you in a difficult real estate transaction. And, of course, there was Michael Jordan, the Most Valuable Person on the team. Michael was the all around go-to-guy, the player who did everything, and when the game got close (which it seldom did), Michael would do something spectacular to change the momentum and assure victory for the team, just like a great real estate broker can do for you. Together the Olympic Dream Team was unbeatable. In the same way, your Home Dream Team can make your home owning efforts unbeatable.

The number of people in the real estate industry that you may encounter can be overwhelming. The following is a list of the people who you may need and their responsibilities. Some of the people will be on your team. Others will be on the seller's team, and some will be on neither team. This list also describes how each player get paid and in whose best interest they play.

Most Important Person

The owner of the Home Dream Team is you. You are the one who pays everyone on your team. The team plays for you, and you are the most important person in the home buying process. Without you, there is no one for the others to support. You are worthy of being treated with respect and dignity at all times. Never let anyone treat you differently. There may be difficult moments ahead, but take time to relax and focus on your goal—to buy a home. Do not constantly measure your self-worth by the opinions of others. Remember Homebuyer Guideline #1: Believe in your power and be powerful in your belief.

Buying your dream house is a personal decision, but having the best professionals supporting you will ensure a more successful and hassle free process. The members on your dream team have roles that will support you in achieving success. It is best to trust each player to do the right thing at the right time under your supervision. You have the final say on what happens with your money.

The following people or institutions that you may need are listed alphabetically. You will be using some or all of their services as you go through the home buying process.

Appraiser

The appraiser is not on your team but is not against your team. The appraiser determines the market value of the house you've chosen based on its condition and the selling price of comparable homes recently sold in the area.

This estimate helps the lender decide a reasonable loan amount for the mortgage. You shouldn't expect an appraiser to uncover a home's defects; that's the inspector's job. The appraiser is someone who verifies to the bank or mortgage company that the property that you are buying is worth the money that you are asking to borrow.

How does an appraiser get paid?

The appraiser's fee is around $300. The lender selects the appraiser, and you will pay this fee at the closing. The appraiser will look at homes in the neighborhood in which the home is located and compare prices for similar size, number of bedrooms and other comparable aspects of homes, in the neighborhood, in which your property is located.

You generally do not have contact with the appraiser. Nevertheless, if you disagree with the appraisal, you can request a copy for your review. If you are not satisfied with the appraisal you can pay for another appraiser to provide a new report.

Commercial Banks and Savings & Loans

This should be one of your first stops in the home buying process. Not only to check for loans, but to step-up checking and savings accounts. Currently African Americans do not patronize commercial banks and savings & loans, especially the black owned and operated financial institutions as often as we should, a situation we cannot afford to continue. Banks and S&Ls deal in conventional lending and have the least expensive loans. These lenders also have the most conservative lending criteria, and if your credit is in bad condition, you may not want to take this route. Nevertheless, a visit to a bank to check on their lending criteria may surprise you. Mortgage brokers primarily work with mortgage banks to secure your loan. Dealing directly with a Commercial lender is perfectly fine. Make sure you get everything in writing or it may cost you money and much aggravation later. Your lender will ask you to fill out a loan application form that includes information about your income, employment and debts. The lender will verify this information. So, be as truthful as your documentation.

How do Banks make their money?

Banks make money from collecting interests on the money they loan and other fees paid by customers.

Contractor

If you decide to buy a new home or have one built to your specifications, you will be working with contractors. In the construction industry, a contractor is one who contracts to erect homes or portions of them. There are also contractors for each phase of construction: heating, electrical, plumbing, etc. There are many stories from homeowners dealing with contractors. Unfortunately, the stories that are repeated most are horror stories of unfinished buildings, or homes constructed from materials that are of lower grade than agreed upon or represented in the selling brochures. This obviously does not reflect the majority of honest and professional contractors. Therefore, you need protection mostly from the incompetent or unethical contractors.

It is almost a given that most building projects will not be completed in the time that is stated. This happens for many reasons that cannot be blamed entirely on the contractors. Building regulations from the state and local governments can be complex and difficult to control for timing. Experienced contractors are aware of this and will include this information in any negotiations. Sometimes building materials that were agreed upon are not available through no fault of the contractor. Again, experienced contractors will have options that are of equal value and quality in reserve.

It is important that when dealing with contractors you do your research and ask around regarding quality of work, timeliness, and work satisfaction from other clients of the contractor. Call your local better business bureau and ask if your contractor has received any complaints. You should also make sure to get everything in writing. It is important that you work with contractors who are established in the community where the home is located. It is less likely that a contractor who is established will risk ruining his reputation by doing shoddy work.

How does a contractor get paid?

Contractors normally make their money by contracted work. A building contractor will sell a home he has made at a percentage over his cost. In the case of new homes, contractors often provide financing to help the homebuyer afford the home. The contractor may add a fee for this service, but in some cases, it is to the contractor's advantage to sell the home, and the contractor will waive fees, and in some cases offer rebates to entice homebuyers to select his homes.

What should I be aware of dealing with contractors?

There are many scams directed to homebuyers and homeowners involving fake or deceitful contractors. One such scam involves offers to build or refinish a home made by a construction company. The procedure seems legit until you pay the large fee, the builders suddenly disappears with your money. It is important that you withhold at least half the payment until you are completely satisfied with work performed. Or you might pay 1/3 at the beginning, 1/3 in the process of the work, and 1/3 of the payment upon satisfactory completion of the job.

Credit Unions

Credit unions are a kind of Savings & Loans. Unlike S&Ls, however, they return any profits to their members. Therefore, they can sometimes offer more advantageous financing.

In the past, credit unions dealt primarily in short-term consumer and auto loans. Nevertheless, during the 1980s the major auto manufacturers began offering their own financing, and this put a dent into the credit unions' ability to find borrowers. As a result, they have turned increasingly to mortgages. Today credit unions offer first and, in some cases, second mortgages. The big catch, of course, is that you must be a member of the credit union in order to borrow from it.

If you belong to a credit union, check out the terms it is offering on mortgages. When compared with other lenders, the credit union may come out looking more favorable. Remember, money is money, and if the credit union gives you a better deal, take it.

How do Credit Unions make their money?

Credit unions make money from collecting interests on the money they loan and other fees.

Escrow or settlement agent

Mutual distrust is the underlying rule of every real estate deal. You and the seller need a neutral third party, an escrow officer, who'll handle funds and paperwork related to the transaction without playing favorites. The escrow officer is the home-buying game's referee.

An escrow agent oversees escrow, the process that some states use to complete a home's sale or purchase. The buyer and seller sign an agreement that gives the escrow agent a detailed list of instructions on how escrow should be carried out, which includes how much money to collect, what documents to prepare and when to order a title search. The escrow agent is a neutral party who fairly represents both the seller and buyer. The escrow agent can be a lender, title company or real estate attorney.

How does an Escrow Agent get paid?

Who pays the settlement fee is a matter of custom depending on the area you are in. If it is customary for the buyer and seller to split this 50-50, that's what the instructions will indicate. Custom notwithstanding, there is no reason you cannot include the following statement in your offer to purchase: "Seller to pay settlement fee."

Fannie Mae and Freddie Mac

You will most likely never deal directly with either Fannie Mae or Freddie Mac. They are major supplier of funds to the lenders who will be providing you with your mortgage, but it is important that you know something about them.

Both Fannie Mae and Freddie Mac are private companies chartered by Congress to provide funds to local lenders for home mortgages in communities all across America. Neither Fannie Mae nor Freddie Mac lends money directly to homebuyers. Instead, both work with lenders to make sure they don't run out of mortgage funds.

Freddie Mac, is a stockholder-owned corporation chartered by Congress in 1970, to create a continuous flow of funds to mortgage lenders in support of homeownership and rental housing.

Fannie Mae is the nation's largest source of financing for home mortgages. A large percentage of African Americans have their loans purchased by Fannie Mae in the secondary market. It is one of the largest financial services corporations in the world. Created by Congress in 1938, to bolster the housing industry in the aftermath of the Great Depression, Fannie Mae was part of the Federal Housing Administration (FHA) and authorized to buy only FHA-insured loans to replenish lenders' supply of money. In 1968, Fannie Mae became a private company operating with private capital on a self-sustaining basis. Its role was expanded to buy mortgages beyond traditional government loan limits, reaching out to a broader cross-section of Americans. Today, Fannie Mae operates under a congressional charter that directs it to channel efforts into increasing the availability and affordability of homeownership for low-, moderate-, and middle-income Americans.

How do Fannie Mae and Freddie Mac make money?

Fannie Mae and Freddie Mac both sell the loans they buy from lenders on the secondary markets to investors, and both make money from financial derivatives that they participate in that are too complicated to answer in this book.

Insurance Agent

When purchasing a home you will also be required to prove that you have homeowners insurance to cover the cost of your home. This is a mandatory condition from lenders. Insurance agencies are in the business of providing this form of coverage to homebuyers. Ask other homeowners or realtors for recommendations on insurance providers.

The insurance agent will offer you various plans, it is to your benefit, and most likely to be required by the lender that you have a full cost replacement policy. This policy states that should your home be destroyed by fire or another catastrophe you and the lender (named as an additional insured party) will be protected financially. The first year's coverage will most likely be included as part of the money you will have to pay at closing, or you will have to present proof that you have a paid up policy.

How does an Insurance Agent get paid?

The fee that you pay and interest earned from your insurance payment pays the insurance. Some insurance officers are independent agents who are able to sell the most effective and appropriate insurance from several insurance agencies to their clients.

What do I need to be aware of when dealing with an Insurance Agent?

Some insurance companies have been reluctant to insure homes for their fair market value, charging African American homeowners more for their insurance, especially if they live in certain areas. This practice is illegal when based solely on the race, color of skin, or religion of a population.

For example, insurance companies are increasingly using credit reports, the history of claims made on a particular property, and the number of claims that an individual has made in a five-year period to determine whether to write a new policy, or not to renew an existing policy. The Foundation for Taxpayers and Consumer Rights takes special exception to the insurance industry's use of credit scoring. "Credit scoring is an abhorrent practice unrelated to insurance, and it should be banned from insurance rating practices," a spokesman for the Foundation stated. Unlike a mortgage or credit card where you are buying access to money and repayment is the issue, with insurance policies, it's security the homeowner is purchasing, and the policy is terminated if the homeowner does not pay.

African American and Hispanic communities are the primary communities affected by this practice, forcing many homeowners into purchasing a Fair Access to Insurance Requirements (FAIR) plan, the last-resort, state-sponsored insurer. But only 29 states have FAIR plans, which vary in coverage depending on the location. Besides being more costly than the voluntary market, FAIR plans often offer less coverage - some covering only fires - and others do not offer full replacement costs.

This issue is especially problematic for African Americans because, according to the U.S. census, 20% of the African American population is concentrated in 10 cities.

If you feel you have been a victim of illegal insurance practice, contact your states attorney general's office and they can direct you to the appropriate insurance regulatory office. Keep accurate records of your interaction with all parties involved to better present your case should it prove necessary.

Loan Officer

Loan officers are employees of the commercial and mortgage banks. Loan officers find customers, sell financial products, and counsel customers. Loan officers employed by mortgage brokers may also be involved in loan processing. In the case of a one-person mortgage broker firm, that person is both the broker and the loan officer.

How does a Loan Officer get paid?

While loan officers are employees, they act more like independent contractors. They are compensated largely, if not entirely, on a commission basis. The typical commission rate is 1/2 of 1% of the loan amount, and successful loan officers earn six figure incomes.

Both lenders and mortgage brokers post prices with loan officers to be offered to consumers. Loan officers usually have limited discretion to reduce the price if necessary to meet competition, and full discretion to raise the price if they can. The difference between the posted price and the price charged the consumer is called an "overage," and it is usually shared with the loan officer.

Reasonably astute shoppers will probably do better dealing with a mortgage broker than with a lender. Because mortgage brokers deal with multiple lenders, they can shop for the best terms available on any given day. In addition, they can find the lenders who specialize in various market niches that many other lenders avoid, such as loans to applicants with poor credit ratings. On the other hand, the risk of encountering a rogue who will trick you into paying more than you should is higher among mortgage brokers than among the loan officer who works for a commercial bank.

Loan Servicer

After the loan closes, the loan servicer collects your payments and manages late payments. Lenders often "release" servicing to another organization, which means that you won't necessarily send your mortgage payments to the same company that made your loan. Your lender will notify you of the correct address for sending your payments.

Who pays a Loan Servicer?

Loan servicers earn a small percentage of the loan payment on each loan they handle. This small percentage adds ups to hundreds of thousands of dollars when combined with the many loans they handle.

Mortgage Banker

A mortgage bankers come in many forms some are very large companies while others are as small as a one-person operation. Mortgage Bankers provide mortgages to a full range of homebuyers and commercial enterprises, often lending to low-, moderate-, and middle-income borrowers needing Federal Housing Administration (FHA) or Veterans Administration (VA) backed financing. For example, Countrywide is one of the countries largest mortgage bankers. Mortgage bankers also bring together providers of capital (investors) and those needing such funds (homebuyers) in all regions of the country.

Servicing more than $2.0 trillion in home mortgages and originating approximately $770 billion in total home mortgages in 1999, mortgage bankers are the leading group of home mortgage lenders, followed by commercial banks, and savings and loans. In 1999, mortgage bankers made home loans as follows (approximately): Conventional, 75 percent, FHA loans, 20 percent, VA loans, 5 percent. Mortgage bankers play a major role in originating loans through the federal government's FHA and VA loan programs. These loan programs are particularly important to low- moderate-, and middle-income homebuyers.

Every year since 1970, mortgage bankers have originated a much larger volume of FHA and VA loans than have other types of lending institutions, consistently providing 80 to 85 percent of all FHA and VA home loans.

Surveys have shown that in comparison to buyers using conventional financing, FHA and VA borrowers are younger, have lower incomes, are two to three times as likely to be first-time homebuyers and purchase homes with much smaller downpayments.

Who pays a Mortgage Banker?

Most mortgage bankers get paid, by the interest they charge you, minus the interest they are charged, for borrowing the money from some other source. A small percentage from your loan payment multiplied by millions of loans amounts to a hefty profit if everything goes well.

Obviously, as a first time homebuyer, you will most likely be working with a mortgage banker, even if you have to go through a mortgage broker to get to one.

Mortgage Broker

The mortgage broker can be one of the most important players on your team if you choose to work with one. You must, however, be vigilant, as there is room for the mortgage broker to pad his fee by charging you more than necessary. People with less then stellar credit often use a mortgage broker. The mortgage broker works with many different banks, and these banks offer the broker a percentage of the price of the loan. The mortgage broker is familiar with the market and should have experience working with people of various incomes and credit histories. Mortgage brokers will have you fill out an application for a fee, and then will shop around for mortgages around the country. Mortgage brokers do not approve or decline loan themselves. Neither do they supply the money for the loan. They are fronts for banks and other lenders.

How does a Mortgage Broker get paid?

When you go to a mortgage broker, the broker sorts through the loan packages offered by various lenders, and helps you choose the right one. For this you pay a fee, usually known as discount points or loan origination points. What may not be clear is that the mortgage broker often receives premiums (money) from the lender. A premium is a fee based on the difference between the rate that the mortgage broker gets for you and the going rate of the loan. The spread between those two numbers determines how much of a premium the broker will get from the lender.

The lender that mortgage brokers deal with quotes a "wholesale" price to the broker, leaving it to the broker to add a markup in order to derive the "retail" price offered the consumer. For example, the wholesale price on a particular program might be 7% and 0 points, to which the broker adds a markup of 1 point, resulting in an offer to the customer of 7% and 1 point. (each point is equal to one percent of the loan amount.) On a $40,000 loan that means the broker gets $400, and on a $300,000 loan, the mortgage broker gets $3,000 not a insignificant amount for approximately the same amount of work as the $40,000 loan. If you increase the mark-up, the fee goes up dramatically. The problem is sometimes mortgage brokers are not upfront about their fee and include it in the writing of the closing costs.

Like any retail business, the mortgage broker adds a markup cost to the mortgage services she provides you. And just like any retail business there is room to negotiate. It is important to understand that a few mortgage brokers are not ethical, and unfortunately, these brokers often seek out the African American community to do business. The illegal or unethical practices that these brokers engage in are difficult to prove, but can be very costly to you.

You have every right to inquire about the mortgage broker's pay-off. Don't become overwhelmed with guilt; remember that your money is lining this person's pockets, and you have every right to know this information.

How do Mortgage Brokers set their markups?

The general rule is that they set them in each case as high as they can get away with. An unsophisticated customer who shows no inclination to shop the competition, will be charged more, than sophisticated customers who make clear their intention to shop around to other mortgage brokers.

Indeed, mortgage brokers often rationalize the high markups they charge some customers, because these are needed to offset the excessively small markups they are forced to accept on other deals. Some borrowers do turn the tables on mortgage brokers by threatening to bail out of a deal after most of the work has been completed, unless the mortgage broker agrees to cut the price.

Some mortgage brokers disclose their fees to customers in advance in writing and disclose the wholesale prices (rates and points) passed through from lenders. These mortgage brokers would get my business.

Questions to ask Mortgage Brokers

1. When I lock the rate/points, will you provide me with a copy of the loan commitment letter as soon as it has been received from the lender?

2. If I elect to float the rate/points, on the day the terms are locked, will you give me the rate/points that are consistent with those being quoted to potential new customers on that day?

An honest mortgage broker would have no problem with this next question. Before accepting any money from me, but after the loan features have been established, will you provide me with the following information in writing.

Mortgage Broker Answer Sheet (examples given)

Type of Loan:	Fixed	(Fixed or adjustable)
Term:	30	Number of Years of Loan
Lock Period:	45	Days (30, 45, 60 days)
Loan Amount:	$60,000	
Interest Rate:	6.25 %	(APR the total cost of loan)
Fee _____	Percent of Loan _____	Dollars $200

Payable to Borrower or the Lender

Application Fee*	$175	Flat fee paid normally paid upfront
Commitment Fee*	$75	Flat fee
Points	1	Based on % of loan
Origination Fee		
Mortgage Broker Fee	1	Based on % of loan
All Other Fees		

Payable to Third Parties

Credit Report Fee	$10	
Appraisal Fee	$200	
Other Fees		
Total		

*Paid before closing. If credited against other fees, deduct from the other fees.

Name of mortgage broker: _____

Signature: _____

If the mortgage broker answers no to any of these questions, then you should not do business with them if possible.

Chapter 2: Making The Dream Home Into Reality

Property/Mechanical Inspector

For a fee, usually in the range of $150 to $400, a qualified inspector will examine the home you've chosen, from basement to attic. The inspection includes an evaluation of the home's plumbing, electrical work, appliances, the furnace and/or air conditioners, roof and structural stability. Some lenders require a home inspection, and it's a good idea to get one, because it could save you thousands of dollars in future expenses. Knowledge of the house's flaws also may help you negotiate a better price on the house.

How does the Property / Mechanical Inspector get paid?

You will be shelling out the money for this service and it is worth it. Be sure to find a creditable inspection company, again ask around or check our website AAHBG.com under service providers.

Real Estate Agent/Broker

The real estate agent or broker (an agent must be supervised by a broker) should be your key player and hopefully your M.V.P. Unlike everyone else, a real estate agent or broker is involved in all aspects of the transaction and should be familiar with all of the players on both the buyer's and seller's team.

The only problem is the traditional real estate agent works on behalf of the seller and will be playing on his teams, which is not in your best interest.

How does the traditional Real Estate Agent get paid?

A real estate agent is paid a commission by the seller, around 6% of the price of house. It is then in the real estate agent's best interest to sell the house at the highest possible price to increase his commission. Legally this real estate agent is responsible to the seller, and any information you give the agent is by law available to the seller. If you told this agent that you really loved the home and would go up another $5,000, the seller's agent is legally and ethically bound to relay this to his client. This situation is obviously not in your best interest.

There is an alternative, and that is hiring a Buyer's Broker.

Picking a Buyers' Broker

If possible, use a buyer's broker, as this will ensure that your real estate agent has your best interest at heart, financially and legally. The official term is fiduciary responsibility, which simply means that the broker is required to be: obedient, loyal, protect your confidentiality, practice fair and honest accounting, and provide full disclosure in all matters pertaining to the purchase of a home that can be of benefit to you. For example, if a seller's agent knew that the seller of a home is willing to lower the price by $5,000, the seller's agent is not under fiduciary responsibility to tell you this information. In difference, a buyer's agent works for you and is required by law to tell you this information.

The main benefit a buyer receives from an agent practicing buyer-brokerage is professionalism and a stronger negotiating position. In 1993, U.S. Sprint found that 232 of its relocating employees using a "buyers' broker" paid an average of 9% below the value of a home's listed price, while those that used a traditional agent paid only 4% lower than the list price. The difference of 5% can be huge financially. If the house was selling for $100,000, 5% comes to a $5,000 savings.

How does a Buyer's Broker get paid?

Typically, a buyer's broker would split the fee that the seller's agent receives. This is called co-brokering and happens frequently. Nevertheless, you should be clear on how your buyer's broker is expecting payment for services rendered after a successful home purchase. This agreement should be written into a contract, detailing all services and other details, such as length of time that the broker would be working with you, number of homes that you should reasonably expect to see in your neighborhood of choice, and other issues. There are some arrangements whereby the buyer pays the buyer's broker upon the completion of the deal. But this is rare.

Ask your friends, co-workers and anyone who has recently bought a home to recommend agents, or you might contact a real estate company in your area. (The classified section of your local newspaper will list real estate companies in the housing section). A real estate professional can show you available houses in a price range that meets your personal needs.

What should I be aware of with a Buyer's Broker?

It is important that your broker is familiar with the neighborhoods that you are considering. There is much information that an informed broker can share if she has contacts in the neighborhoods, such as the quality of the schools, services available in the communities and the overall safety of the neighborhood. A real estate broker would know the prices of homes in the area and can help advise you on the price you should offer.

After you find a home, your agent should handle all negotiations with the seller. You should have established a clear and trusting relationship with your broker, as she is often the person who can make or break your deal with the seller.

If you are not comfortable with your broker, then you should not hesitate to get another broker. However, if it doesn't look like your broker is doing anything for the money he or she receives, that is not normally the case. Most of the broker's work is out of your sight. Brokers visit many homes alone looking for their client's needs and desires. Brokers are constantly browsing the newspapers and websites to find properties. The brokers have other contacts that can help locate properties that might not be available through other means. Brokers have worked with many homebuyers and understand the anxiety, impatience, and emotions that come with the home buying process.

Questions to ask a Real Estate Agent/Broker

Before you sign anything, confirm your needs to the real estate agent and ask specific questions such as:

1. Has the agent sold a home to an African American in the past year?

2. How does the agent place clients in regards to neighborhoods?

3. Does the agent's firm also handle seller listings?

4. Does your agent place equal emphasis on all available homes (including for sale by owners), which meet your needs and wants?

5. What does the home buying process mean to this agent?

6. Ask the agent how long he or she has been a realtor. Ask about his most difficult experience with a buyer client and how he handled it?

7. Can the agent give you referrals or testimonials from past clients?

8. Find out if the agents have an assistant and what that person's duties are in relation to your purchase.

These few questions should be asked. If you don't like the answers you get, don't hesitate to continue looking until you find a realtor with whom you are comfortable.

Real Estate Attorney

Real estate transactions in some states require by law the use of a real estate attorney. If you have any questions about the legality of your contract, get a lawyer on your team as soon as possible. No one else on the team is legally qualified to give you legal advice.

If you are buying a home in a state that requires a lawyer, such as New York, then you have little choice in accepting a lawyer's services. In states that do not require a lawyer, it may be to your benefit to hire one. You need a lawyer any time you get into a situation that isn't covered by a standard contract. Unless your agent is also a lawyer, he or she isn't qualified to do creative legal writing. A lawyer should handle complicated issues, such as those that frequently arise from partnership agreements between unrelated people who buy property together, and the complex legal ramifications of taking title to your home. The lawyer can write legally binding documents including amendments to your purchase agreements. Lawyers can do title searches or even handle the closing. Closing can be held at an attorney's office.

When no real estate broker is involved, such as in a for-sale-by-owner transaction, you should have a lawyer look over the contract. If neither you nor the seller has an agent, get a lawyer to prepare the contract and have the lawyer do the work that an agent would normally handle. Eliminating an agent doesn't eliminate the need for disclosures, inspections, contingency removals, and a myriad of other details involved in the home buying process.

The attorney should be familiar with real estate law for the state in which the property is located, and it is even better if that was his main practice. You should trust your lawyer 100%. Therefore, it is important that you select one that is honest and sincere. Ask your friends and co-workers for referrals. Remember a lawyer who is right for someone else may not be right for you. Don't rush into a commitment just to please your friends or co-worker.

How is an Attorney paid?

You are responsible for paying Attorney fees, which can be expensive. The lawyer can request to be paid upfront (which I do not recommend that you do with anyone), or half before and after the closing (better), or payment in full at the closing (best). Find a lawyer who gives an estimate, and if possible a written estimate, detailing normal and expected costs. Many unusual situations do arise, but a good lawyer will notify you before charging. The cost for a lawyer ranges anywhere from between $250 to $1,200 depending on the state, complexity of the transaction and other factors.

Joanie had a flat fee situation with her lawyer whom she would call often and for the smallest question. She was upset that her lawyer was always abrupt on the phone. Joanie was on the verge of getting another lawyer when she found out that her current lawyer normally charged $300 per hour, including phone calls. After that, Joanie was the one who was abrupt on the phone.

Questions to ask a lawyer

- What is your experience in this field?
- What are your rates and how often will you bill me?

- What is a ballpark figure for the total bill, including fees and expenses?
- How will you keep me informed of progress?
- Who else in the office will be working on my home purchase deal?
- Can junior attorneys or paralegals in the office handle some of the administrative work at a lower rate?
- Can you be reached on Fridays, Holidays and weekends?
- How many other homebuyers have you assisted in buying a home?
- Will you be at the closing, or will you send a paralegal or assistant?

State or Local Housing Finance Agency

Some government agencies provide valuable housing assistance to low- and moderate-income homebuyers and renters. To find out more about these programs, ask your real estate agent or lender. Some states provide mortgage financing or financial support in emergencies for homeowners. To contact your state's or local housing agencies check your telephone directory or the internet.

Seller

The Seller is the person, agency, or building company from which you will be buying your home. The seller is attempting to receive as much money as possible from the sale of their property.

How does the Seller get paid?

From you if you pay cash. If you are borrowing the money, a lender pays the seller. You will sign your home over to the lender; until you pay back the money, the lender gave the seller.

What do I need to be aware of in dealing with a Seller?

In some cases, a seller is not reasonable about the price of his or her home, or may not want to sell. That happens all the time. Don't take it personally. When negotiating with a reluctant seller, it is important to have confidence in your real estate agent, as she will be doing the negotiating. If you feel, sense or absolutely know that racism has entered into the negotiations, don't confront the seller. Speak to your real estate agent. Discuss your feelings clearly until you are sure you are being heard. An honest real estate agent knows that racism rears its pervasive head and may have the skill to deal with it. During a situation like this, you must consider whether or not if the seller is a reflection of the neighborhood, and if so, do you want to come home everyday for the next ten years or more to that type of environment. How would your children react? I don't have an answer either way. Sometimes you make a decision based on your heart, and you must go with it. Other times a carefully thought out and planned decision is the best way.

When dealing with racism, there are very few set answers other than to know that you are not the problem.

Support Person

Pro sport teams hire cheerleaders to encourage the players when the situation is difficult and uncertain and to celebrate after victory has been won, and so should you. Your support person or people can be made up of a husband or wife, friends or family. Include someone who is currently a homeowner if possible. Relying on these people when the times are tough will make stressful situations seem much lighter. Your support team should be good listeners and be very positive people who have your best interest at heart. Buying a home can take many months, and there will be times that it may seem like years, so it is important that your support person be around for the long haul and has a good understanding of your strengths and weaknesses. Your support team should like and respect you, and you should like and respect them.

Maxwell a new homeowner shared this experience. At a crucial moment in Maxwell's home buying process, the owner of the building decided to quit the sale. Maxwell was crushed and angry, three months of time and money wasted. Maxwell called his cousin Keira, his support person and a homeowner. Keira listened for three hours on the various evils of the owner. Afterwards, Keira recalled an episode from Maxwell's childhood. Maxwell wanted to buy a bicycle and patiently saved $1.50 a week for a whole year. Keira reminded Maxwell of how she was impressed by Maxwell's consistency and perseverance then, and Keira was sure that Maxwell still had those traits. This encouraged Maxwell to make another effort, and sure enough, the owner reconsidered and decided to go through with the sale. Find your support person first, and the rest of the team will come together as a matter of course.

How does the Support Person get paid?

Ideally, the support person is someone who has a personal investment in you becoming a homeowner and thus is not looking for any monetary gain. No one likes to be taken for granted, so remember to take care of your support team(s) as if they had performed a paying service. Take them out to dinner and provide appropriate gifts during difficult times. It will strengthen the bond between you and them.

What to be aware of with your Support Person?

Your support people may be around longer than your first home so always be considerate and listen to their advice.

This covers the primary people and agencies normally associated with a home purchase. You may have an opportunity to deal with other people not included above. Remember they all exist to help you buy a home and without you their would be nothing for them to do.

Where we've been

At this point, you should have organized your Home-in-a-box filing system. You should have an understanding of some of the people you will be meeting in the process of buying your home. In the next chapter, we begin determining your financial situation.

Affirmation

I am giving positive people, positive energy, and I will receive positive results.

Chapter 3
SHOW ME THE MONEY

"I started saving when I was a little girl just to have candy money. When I got grown, I started saving for my future. I'd go to the bank once a month, hold out just enough to cover my expenses and put the rest into my saving account."

—Osceola McCarthy, 1908- , Housekeeper and Philanthropist

"In the first place, we need to obtain economic independence. You may talk about rights and all that sort of thing. The people who own this country will rule this country. They always have done so and they always will."

—Carter G. Woodson, 1875 – 1950, Historian

Patrice and Anthony Thomason celebrated their fourth wedding anniversary by cutting up thirteen credit cards. They then opened two savings accounts, and began investing a portion of their salary in a 401K plan. This anniversary was far different from their second; in which they spent $2,300, they could not afford on a cruise to Bermuda. At that time, neither Anthony nor Patrice had any idea of their true financial situation. Borrowing from credit cards to pay their bills, and paying the minimum due at the end of the month was their idea of financial planning. This changed when Anthony was laid off from his job, and for a year, they endured repossession hell. Anthony shares the experience, "First, they came and took my high priced foreign recording equipment. Then they came for our beautiful and expensive furniture, and lastly our convertible sports car." Patrice added, "By the end of 2000, after borrowing from family and friends, we were left with nothing but a half empty apartment and cereal for breakfast, lunch, and dinner. We finally decided to get help." They began by calling a financial planner and placing themselves on a strict budget. Anthony took several part-time jobs, and Patrice added another job on the weekends. It took two years for their effort to pay off. Now, left with only two thousands dollars of credit debt, they have decided to make managing their finances a priority commitment to themselves and their marriage. They are planning on buying a home by the end of this year.

Where We're Going In This Chapter

Before you rush out to look for your Dream Home, you need to know how much home rather than dream you can afford. You don't want to spend your precious time and money looking at homes that are out of your price range. That means knowing how much money you have available for the necessities of life, such as mortgage or rent, food, education, healthcare and so on.

In this chapter, you will get your financial house in order. A process that is tedious, but necessary, if you wish to buy a home you can keep in good times and bad. We will determine how much money you have right now, that can be put towards a home. You will pre-qualify yourself using the same criteria that the lenders use. You will also review your credit by ordering your credit report and correcting negative issues that may prevent you from being approved for a mortgage. We will also breakdown the costs of owning a home. Finally, you will be encouraged to visit a lender to be pre-approved for a mortgage.

Getting Pre-qualified vs. Pre-approved

When you're under contract to buy a property, having your mortgage application denied during the crucial period after the purchase contract has been signed, may cause you to lose the property. Losing a home that you've spent weeks or months searching for, and a great deal of emotional energy to secure, can be devastating. Some sellers won't be willing to wait for you to go through another four weeks or more to get another mortgage, especially if they need to sell quickly. If the sellers have other buyers waiting in the wings, you've likely lost the property.

How can you avoid this? Pre-qualification and pre-approval.

I recommend going on-line to *www.finance.com* and pre-qualifying yourself. It painless and free. You can try several scenarios to see what your chances are for getting a loan. If you don't want to deal with the internet you can call or visit a lender in person and they should be excited to help you. The lender would then provide an opinion of the loan amount that you can borrow based solely on what you, the borrower, tell the lender. The lender doesn't verify anything and is not bound to make the loan when you're ready to buy.

Pre-approval is a much more rigorous process, which is why I prefer it to pre-qualification. Loan pre-approval is based on documented and verified information regarding your likelihood of continued employment, your income, your liabilities, and the cash you have available to close on a home purchase.

The only thing the lender can't pre-approve is the property you intend to buy, because of course, you haven't found it yet.

Going through the pre-approval process is a sign of your seriousness to house sellers. A lender's pre-approval letter is considerably stronger than a pre-qualification letter. In a multiple-offer situation where more than one prospective buyer bids on a home, buyers who have been pre-approved have an advantage over buyers who aren't.

Lenders don't normally charge for pre-qualification. Some lenders don't charge for a pre-approval, but many do, and a pre-approval does not last indefinitely, normally, for at most 90 days. If you do plan on getting pre-approved and it is going to cost you money, then make sure you're quite certain you will be buying a home soon or you may pay for the pre-approval only to lose the money. For a pre-approval you will need to bring all of your documentation and a check or money order for the fee.

> The average white household has a net worth of $84,000. The average black household has only about $7,500.
>
> If there were full racial equality in America, the wealth of black households would rise by $1 trillion.
>
> African Americans would have $200 billion more in the stock market, $120 billion more in pension plans, and $80 billion more in the bank. And there might be 31 African American billionaires instead of three.
>
> From a speech given by Franklin Raines to the Urban League in 2001.

The Costs Of Purchasing A House

Pre-approval can be expensive, and it is important to know the other costs involved in buying and owning a home. The costs involved in purchasing a house include both upfront costs and ongoing expenses.

Upfront costs

Upfront costs are the monies you will be expected to pay before you own the home. These costs include loan application fees, the down payment, closing (or settlement) costs.

Down payment. Nearly everyone who purchases a house must rely on a loan from a bank or other lender. Most lenders require that you contribute a portion of the purchase price of the home from your own funds so that you have a personal investment in the property. Lack of down payment money is one of the primary factors contributing to African Americans not completing the steps to becoming a homeowner. Where to get help (money) is explained in detail in the appendix.

Traditionally, buyers are expected to make a down payment of 20 percent of the purchase price. For example, if you were buying a $60,000 house, you would have to make a $12,000 down payment from your own money and borrow the remaining $48,000. Today, buyers may be able to pay as little as 3 to 5 percent of the purchase price (or in some cases even less) as a down payment. A 5 percent down payment on a $60,000 home would be $3,000, while a 3 percent down payment would be $1,800. You would then borrow $57,000 and $58,200 respectively.

Low- and moderate-income homebuyers may be eligible for grants or subsidized loans that can be used to increase the size of their down payment, thereby reducing the mortgage amount (and the monthly mortgage payments). Sources of supplemental financing are discussed in detail at the end of this chapter. The organizations that provide help and in some cases gifts in the form of non-repaid loans or matching funds are presented in the appendix.

Closing costs. Both homebuyers and home sellers are responsible for a number of costs that must be paid when the mortgage closes. The buyers' closing costs generally range from 2 to 6 percent of the total mortgage amount, which can be amount to a quite a bit of money. For example, if you were to buy a $247,000 you could expect to pay closing costs of around $5,000 to almost $15,000. If the loan amount is $50,000 you would be paying around $1, 000 to $3,000. This is in addition to the down payment. In some cases, individuals or organizations other than the borrower may pay the closing costs. The seller could agree to pay the closing cost in order to sell the home sooner.

Settling-in costs and needed repairs. You should consider how much money you would need to settle into your new house. Besides the actual cost of moving, you may need to purchase appliances and furniture. This is not the time to spend hundreds of dollars just to have new appliances. Buy what is only necessary and shop for bargains. Houses are generally purchased "as is", so the buyer is responsible for making any needed repairs. You should also be prepared to pay fees for hooking up or transferring the utilities (such as telephone, cable TV, electricity, and gas or oil service) to your own account.

Ongoing costs

In addition to these initial costs of homeownership, there are ongoing costs. These are monies you will have to spend each month or yearly for as long as you are a homeowner. The monthly mortgage payment, utility bills, property taxes, maintenance costs, and homeowner's and mortgage insurance premiums. In addition, condominium owners pay a monthly condo fee.

Monthly mortgage payment. The amount of a borrower's monthly mortgage payment depends on the amount borrowed, the term (the number of years that you make payments) of the loan, and the interest rate. Each mortgage payment is allocated first to repay the accrued interest (the fee charged for borrowing funds), with the remainder going to reduce the principal (the amount borrowed).

Taxes and insurance. Monthly mortgage payments often include an added amount that the lender uses to pay for property taxes, homeowner's insurance, and mortgage insurance (MI), or private mortgage insurance (PMI), if your loan is FHA government insured. The lender holds these collected funds in a separate escrow account and pays the tax and insurance bills when they come due. In this way, the lender ensures that these important expenses are paid on time. If taxes and insurance are not included in the monthly mortgage, you must be prepared to pay these bills when they come due.

Since taxes and insurance (T&I) are an essential part of a homeowner's housing costs, lenders often refer to the components of a mortgage payment as "PITI" (an abbreviation for principal, interest, taxes, and insurance).

Condo/co-op fees. If you purchase a unit in a condominium or cooperative, you will pay a monthly condominium or cooperative fee, which goes toward the upkeep of the common areas.

Utilities. The cost of utilities (oil, gas, electricity, and water) is an expense that may vary considerably throughout the year (increasing during the heating season, for example). Some strategies for reducing these costs are described in Chapter 7.

Maintenance and repairs. First-time homebuyers are often surprised by how expensive the cost for basic home upkeep, both in terms of time and money. Emergency repairs (such as fixing a leaky roof or a backed-up toilet) represent unexpected expenses. Financial advisers suggest that homeowners put aside 5 percent of their monthly income in a maintenance fund (for example, $50 per month if your monthly income is $1,000) until you have built up a reserve equal to three to six months' worth of housing expenses.

These are the primary and basic costs to homeownership. There may be additional fees and expenses that are unique to your own situation.

Understanding Lender's Loan Qualifications

Lenders determine whether to approve a loan by looking at the borrowers' Capacity, Credit history, Capital, and Collateral. Be sure you understand the importance of each of these elements. The lender looks at the borrowers' monthly earnings from employment or other stable sources of income such as public benefits, or a combination of both — Capacity. The lender will then look at the loan applicants' past borrowing record to see if they paid their debts and bills on time — Credit history. The lender wants to know that the borrower has enough cash for a down payment and closing costs — Capital. The lender wants to be protected if the borrower fails to repay the loan — Collateral.

Assets Worthsheet

Use the following Asset Worthsheet to determine how much money you have available for a down payment.

Assets	Borrower	Co-Borrower	Total
ASSETS FOR DOWNPAYMENT WORTHSHEET			
Savings account	$	$	$
Checking account	$	$	$
Cash value of life insurance	$	$	$
Proceeds from sale of current home, if applicable	$	$	$
Gift from relatives*	$	$	$
Other assets that can be sold to obtain funds (cars,	$	$	$
A. Total Assets	$	$	$
Liabilities			
Moving expenses (movers, truck rental)			$
New home repairs (plumbing, wiring)			$
Home decorating			$
Major appliance purchases			$
Estimated closing costs at settlement (usually 3 – 6% of your loan amount)			$
Other major purchases in next six months unrelated to new home (car, education, etc)			$
B. Total Liabilities			$
Total Assets $_____ – Total Liabilities $_____ = Downpayment $_____			

* Some mortgages put a limit on how large a gift you can use for your down payment. Check with your lender to determine exact amounts and appropriate forms to complete.

** Remember, lenders may require you to have two months of mortgage payments in reserve when you go to closing. Be sure to consider this in your cash needs for the next six months.

With a maximum down payment in mind, you now can figure the next factor that will affect your monthly mortgage payments: which is the amount of money you borrow.

Your actual mortgage payments will depend in large part on the amount you borrow – that is called the mortgage principal. Your income and your debts are the most important factors for determining how large a mortgage you will be able to get. If you are buying a house with someone else (spouse, parent, adult child, partner/companion, friend, brother, sister, etc.), you should consider your co-purchaser's earnings and existing debts as well. If you apply for a loan with somebody else, you and your co-borrower are both legally responsible for repayment of the mortgage.

Lender Qualifying Ratios

Lenders have traditionally used qualifying ratios as an important tool in determining the likelihood that a loan applicant will be able to repay the mortgage. Lenders generally use the following two qualifying guidelines (often referred to as ratios). The most common ratios for conventional mortgages (not insured by government agencies) are 28% and 36%.

- The first guideline says that a borrower should spend no more than 28 percent of their gross monthly income (income before taxes) on monthly housing expenses. Monthly housing expenses include mortgage principal and interest, hazard insurance, real estate taxes, and private mortgage insurance (if applicable). Lenders do not include monthly utility bills in your monthly housing expense ratio;

- The second guideline says that a borrower's monthly housing expenses and other long term debts combined generally should not be more than 36 percent of total monthly income. That means that your monthly mortgage principal and interest payments, real estate taxes, hazard insurance, car loan, credit card payments, and other long-term debts combined generally may not exceed 36 percent of your gross monthly income.

These ratios (28 percent of total income for housing expenses and 36 percent for total debt) are flexible guidelines. If you have a consistent record of paying rent that is very close in amount to your proposed monthly mortgage payment or you make a large down payment, you may be able to convince your lender to accept a somewhat higher ratio. What's more, some lenders offer special loan programs for lower and moderate-income homebuyers. Allowing as much as 33 percent of their gross monthly income to be used toward housing expenses and 38 percent for total debt, and in some areas where real estate is extremely high even higher ratios are accepted.

Total Gross Income

Use the following Gross Monthly Income Worksheet to calculate the total gross (before-tax) monthly income for you and your co-borrower; if you have one. Be sure you include all the income your household receives on a regular basis, indicating any monies received under each item listed.

GROSS MONTHLY INCOME WORKSHEET			
Monthly Income (before taxes)	**Borrower**	**Co-Borrower**	**Total**
1. Salary 1st Job	$	$	$
2. Salary 2nd Job			
3. Overtime *			
4. Bonuses *			
5. Commissions *			
6. Dividends/Interest			
7. Alimony/Child Support			
8. Unemployment Compensation			
9. Pension/Social Security Benefits			
10. Public Assistance/Food Stamps			
11. Veterans Benefits			
12. Other Income			
13. Total Gross Monthly Income			$
* If your overtime, bonuses, or commissions do not fall into 12 equal monthly payments, be sure to divide them to spread this income over 12 months. You will need to a two-year history of receipts for this income to rent.			

28% of Total Income Ratio Calculation

Multiply your Total Gross Monthly Income above by 28 percent to get the maximum allowable housing expense.

14. Your Total Gross Monthly Income (from table above) $ _____

15. Multiply by 28%   x .28

16. This is the maximum amount you should spend each month for housing. $ _____

Long Term Monthly Household Debt Worksheet

Use the following to total your existing loans, alimony, student loans, car payments, and other monthly payments on long-term debts below. Be sure to disclose all the long-term debts of each co-borrower.

LONG TERM MONTHLY HOUSEHOLD DEBT WORKSHEET		
Please enter minimum monthly payment required on each of your outstanding debts	Borrower	Co-Borrower
17. Total installment and revolving debts (credit cards)	$	$
18. Car loan		
19. Student loans		
20. Existing real estate loans (if you are **not** selling the property)		
21. Alimony/Child support that you pay		
22. Other long-term monthly debts (including loans from relatives, loan against insurance policy)		
23. **Add all the debts above to calculate your Monthly Debt**	$	
24. Include your Allowable Housing Expense on line 16 from the previous page	$	
25. **Add Line 23 and 24 to get your Total Monthly Debt**	$	
* Note: Ongoing monthly living expenses you pay for in cash such as utility payments; grocery bills; entertainment expenses; and health, life medical, and car insurance are not considered long-term debts for mortgage loan qualifying purposes		

Calculate your maximum allowable long-term monthly debt

26. Your Total Gross Monthly Income (from table #2) $ _____

27. Multiply by 36% x .36

28. Equals the maximum amount of money you should spend on housing and other debts _____

29. Take the amount from line 25. $ _____

30. Subtract line 29 from line 28. If positive you may qualify for a loan. If negative you need to adjust your spending or income. $ _____

Maximum Allowable Income and Debt Chart

The following chart estimates how high your monthly housing expenses and your long-term monthly debt can be based on your income. "Allowable monthly housing expense" includes mortgage principal and interest, property taxes, hazard insurance, and, if applicable, mortgage insurance.

ALLOWABLE MONTHLY HOUSING EXPENSE AND MONTHLY DEBT BASED ON YOUR INCOME			
Gross Income		Allowable Monthly Ratio	
Annual	Monthly	28% Total Housing	36% Total Debt
$20,000	$1,667	$467	$600
25,000	2,083	583	750
30,000	2,500	700	900
35,000	2,917	817	1,050
40,000	3,333	933	1,200
45,000	3,750	1,050	1,350
50,000	4,167	1,167	1,500
55,000	4,583	1,283	1,650
60,000	5,000	1,400	1,800
65,000	5,417	1,517	1,950
70,000	5,833	1,633	2,100
75,000	6,250	1,750	2,250
80,000	6,667	1,867	2,400
85,000	7,083	1,983	2,550
90,000	7,500	2,100	2,700
95,000	7,917	2,217	2,850
100,000	8,333	2,333	3,000
120,000	10,000	2,800	3,600
140,000	11,667	3,267	4,200
160,000	13,333	3,733	4,800
180,000	15,000	4,200	5,400
200,000	16,667	4,667	6,000

To use the chart above, find your annual/monthly gross salary. Then in the 28% or 36% column find the corresponding allowable amount.

If you know how much you will need to borrow (the purchase price minus your down payment) and what interest rate the lender will charge, you can use the principal and interest (P&I) calculator located in the appendix. It is called the "How Much Is It – Finder". To determine the monthly principal and interest payment on a standard 30-year fixed-rate mortgage.

Improving your ratios

If your qualifying ratios exceed 42 percent, you are not likely to qualify for any mortgage, nor should you want to. To strengthen your financial profile, you must be able to document additional qualifying income, less debt, or lower housing costs. As a rule of thumb, for every $50 of "excess debt", you can expect about a $5,000 reduction in the amount of mortgage for which you might qualify. If your debts are excessive, consider paying off some of these debts in preparation for buying a house. Or you may want to consider accepting a smaller mortgage that would enable you to purchase a more modest home.

Keep in mind that you may be eligible for gifts, grants, or subsidized second mortgages that could reduce the size of the first mortgage (and result in lower monthly payments). These resources, which may make homeownership more feasible, are described in the Increasing Your Borrowing Power of this chapter.

Analyzing your credit as part of your pre-qualifying for a mortgage

For many African Americans the single largest obstacle to buying a home is the *fear* of bad credit. Regardless of the reality, most African Americans either don't know their credit situation or assume it is far worse than it actually is. It is vital that you are aware of your credit record that is being reported to lenders. This report is sent from the credit reporting agencies to lenders to evaluate your record of payment.

Credit Report Factors

Mortgage lenders use the information contained in your credit report as part of the underwriting process. The credit report factors considered include: credit history, delinquent accounts, credit card accounts, public records, foreclosures, collection accounts, and inquiries. Each characteristic is weighed based on the amount of risk and its significance to the underwriting recommendation. Your credit behavior is assessed over a long period. Therefore, short-term attempts to improve your credit record, such as paying off an account or closing an account, may not always have a positive impact on your credit record.

Credit History

Your credit history is an account of how well you handle credit, both now and in the past. Generally, the longer you've had an established credit history, the better. An older, established account—even one with a zero balance—might have more positive impact on your credit report than a newly established account. Having a relatively new credit history (a few recently opened accounts) is not automatically considered a higher credit risk. Making payments on time on newly established accounts signifies less risk than not making payments on time on older accounts. You may not have any established credit history. For instance, you may not have the type of credit that is typically reported to a credit bureau. This does not mean you will be unable to get a mortgage. You may be able to work with your mortgage lender using your payment history on such items as rent and utilities to establish a "nontraditional" credit history. In those cases, your lender will need to separately assess your credit history and its impact on the overall risk of your loan.

Credit Scoring

A number of lenders are relying on a different system of rating your risk level, called FICO credit score. It is called FICO due to the fact that Fair, Isaac and Company created the system. The typical scoring is in the range of 350 – 800+. Scores lower than 620 almost eliminates your chances of getting a loan from a conventional lender, on the other hand if your score is above 720 you should qualify for a prime interest rate loan. Studies have shown that even with high credit ratings many African Americans are given higher interest rates than white Americans with similar scores and financial situations. Therefore, you must be vigilant with any lender even if you have an excellent credit rating. The following table shows the general credit status and the resulting mortgage decision.

FICO Score	Credit Rating	Mortgage Credit Decision
Over 800	A+	Lenders usually salivate over these scores. Visit several and demand the best rates, because you got it like that.
720-799	A - A-	You should still get a great rate. If you don't, ask why and possibly look elsewhere.
660-719	A- - B	Still very good, unless you declared a bankruptcy.
620-659	B- - C	Lenders will begin to be leery. So, you will have to look harder. You still can find a conventional loan.
619 and below	C- - D	This is FHA or subprime territory. Don't worry you are not alone; you will get very high rates, consider improving your score by handling your business with your creditors.

Prime interest rate vs. Sub-prime rate

The Prime Rate is the interest rate charged by banks to their most creditworthy customers (usually the most prominent and stable business customers). The prime rate or A credit is usually the same amongst major banks. Adjustments to the prime rate are generally made by banks at the same time, although, the prime rate does not adjust on any regular basis. Sub-prime rate B, C or D credit is the more costly rate that banks charge borrowers with less than perfect credit. There is no objective standard to who receives the prime and sub-prime rate. Credit scores are not the only measurement; which makes it difficult to hold lenders to a measurable benchmark. For example, if the prime rate is listed in the daily paper at 6.25% a borrower with excellent credit should receive a loan at this 6.25%. But a crafty lender might say that your work history is not stable therefore you will get a higher interest rate.

Credit Card Accounts

Avoid overextended credit. Credit cards are tools that can be used to establish good credit. You can use credit cards to show how you manage credit wisely, either by paying off the balances every month or by keeping them very low. But, it is possible to get into unhealthy debt by overusing or misusing your credit cards. There are two types of credit card accounts—revolving credit card accounts and 30-day accounts. A revolving credit card account does not require immediate repayment of the credit charge. Instead, you are only responsible for a minimum monthly payment—usually a small percentage of your balance. A 30-day account is one that requires payment of the full balance within 30 days. The amount of credit you have and how you use it are important. When you use all of your available credit, there is a good chance that you may be overextended. Therefore, when the total amount of debt owed on all of your open credit card accounts is close to the credit limits, this indicates higher risk.

Here are some telltale signs that you may be carrying too much debt:

_____   Do you have balances that never seem to drop?

_____   Are your balances getting higher?

_____   Do you regularly make low or minimum payments?

_____   Do you juggle bill payments?

In addition to getting pre-qualified for a mortgage before you begin house hunting, you should also obtain a copy of your credit report from each of the three major credit bureaus. Lenders rely heavily on individual credit reports to determine whether loan applicants have a history of paying their bills regularly and on time.

Accessing Credit Reports

Because each of the three major credit bureaus collects slightly different credit information, you need to examine all three reports. To order your credit reports, you should contact:

- Equifax (www.equifax.com) - Telephone: 1-800-685-1111
- Experian (www.experian.com) - Telephone 1-888-397-3742
- Trans Union (www.transunion.com)-Telephone 1-800-916-8800.

Credit bureaus may charge a small fee for credit reports, although in many states individuals may obtain one free copy per year. When someone is denied credit because of a poor credit history, they can request a copy of their credit report free of charge. Various form letters you can use to submit requests from the credit agencies are located at the end of this chapter.

Correcting an Erroneous Credit Record

If you find any errors in your credit reports or believe they give a misleading picture of past credit problems that have been resolved, you should attempt to get them corrected before applying for a mortgage. You do this by writing directly to the credit bureau and asking for an investigation of any items you believe are incorrect. The credit bureau must investigate and respond within 30 days. If an error is still not corrected, the credit bureau will explain what steps need to be taken. If you continue to disagree with any portion of your credit report, the credit bureau must include your explanation of the situation in future reports. There are form letters that you may use as samples to send to the credit agencies located at the end of this chapter.

Repairing a Bad Credit Record

Your credit report may reflect the fact that you did not always pay your bills in a timely manner. If you are currently having credit problems, you may not be in a position to buy a house until these issues are resolved. To proceed would only add to your problems. You might be denied a loan or be offered a sub-prime loan with significantly higher interest rates and fees to offset the lender's higher risk.

10 Credit Scams That Affect African Americans

I have been the victim of a credit scam and I am not ashamed to mention it. It wasn't my fault, well maybe it was anyway you may have been also. There are so many scams in this techno world of ours it is difficult to keep up. These scams are most effective when you are in need of quick cash or when the devilish nature of greed has emerged from within your heart. The thought of free money or beating the system is often the impetus for reaching for the phone to call the number you just heard on the radio or seen on T.V. at 3:00 am. The people behind these scams know that even if you don't call your neighbor will. They work on percentages and the percentage of our people who need quick cash is too high.

These are just a few that affect all Americans as well as African Americans in particular. When dealing with people over the telephone or in any situation that requires you to provide your personal information, such as social security number, credit card number or even your telephone number, be skeptical, and ask questions. A good one question to ask in a semi-joking manner is "You aren't trying to scam me are you?" sometimes the person will tell you yes, and you should believe them. More often they will answer no, and you should be even more wary.

The following list is from the internet type in credit scams and African Americans and you might get a list similar to this or maybe a little different, this list is not all-inclusive or in any particular order.

1. **Phony Credit Repair Companies** – Credit-repair companies run advertisements in newspapers, radio, TV, and the Internet, offering consumers assistance, for a price, to clean up their credit histories. The Federal Trade Commission (FTC) warns that many of the claims these companies make—that they can remove judgments, liens, and other unfavorable information from credit records, are false. They cannot legally remove accurate negative information from a credit report and any legitimate help they can offer can be pursued by consumers themselves, at little or no cost.

2. **Telephone credit scams** – Here 900 or 976 numbers are leased from the phone companies by other companies that want to sell you a product or service by phone. Calling these numbers, you pay an additional charge above the normal call costs. This charge can top 20 dollars per minute! How does this relate to your credit? Credit is the item most commonly advertised by companies who use these 900 or 976 phone numbers. They may invite you to call their number to obtain a secured bankcard or catalogue credit card. Bu all you then receive for your money is a credit application–plus a very large phone bill.

3. **Advance fee loans** – The lenders appeal to consumers who, based on their credit history, can't get a loan. The scammers falsely promise that for an advance payment, even consumers with bad credit histories can get a loan. Some of these lenders make money through the 900 numbers that charge consumers who call to find out about the loans. Others simply charge consumers a fee for a loan that is never delivered.

4. **File segregation** – This is a relatively new scam that could get you fined or sentenced to jail time if you use it. It is an illegal scheme used by credit-repair companies to encourage consumers with unfavorable credit histories to obtain new taxpayer identification or employer identification numbers from the Internal Revenue Service under false pretenses and use them to hide their true credit identities from creditors. For a fee, the companies promise advice on how to go about segregating their credit files. File segregation is illegal and consumers who employ it are committing a felony.

5. **Second mortgage scams** – These are most common to the home improvement industry where con men offer to make home improvements in poor neighborhoods to people with considerable equity in their homes. They are always prime targets of this scam. The contractor arranges financing for his victims with lenders who offer second mortgages with very high interest rates and loan origination fees. Sometimes a contractor can convince the homeowner to sign a trust deed to secure the work on the home. Even if the owner is dissatisfied with the work, the contractor can force the sale of the home to collect his money.

6. **Bait and switch conversion loans** – Here unscrupulous loan brokers offer you a below market rate mortgage. If you first accept a mortgage loan with very high interest, you are promised that it will be converted to a lower interest mortgage. But until that happens you must continue to pay the interest. Beware. Conversion to the low-interest loan seldom happens.

7. **Mortgage reduction information kits** – These expensive kits that cost hundreds of dollars, and are peddled door to door, contain no information that you cannot find elsewhere free or a few dollars. They all tell you the same thing; cut your mortgage payments into bi-weekly installments to save interest! The problem is that only a few banks will accept bi-weekly payments.

8. **Pre-payment penalties** – This costly provision, usually found in the fine print of a loan agreement, is designed to keep you forever in debt.

If you should fully pay the loan before it is due, the lender then forces you to pay a penalty. To pay a 5 percent penalty of the remaining $50,000 on your mortgage, will cost you an extra $2,500. Negotiate this out of the contract! Also, find out if your state restricts this type of clause. Many do.

9. **Uncapped variable interest rates** – These are also dangerous to your financial health. A capped variable interest rate is an interest rate that fluctuates with the prime interest rate, but never rises above a certain point. In contrast, an uncapped variable rate may start at nine percent, but with no ceiling, can rise to 20 percent or more as happened in the early 1980s. Variable rates are always dangerous, but this type of rate leaves you without any protection whatsoever.

10. **Invasion of privacy** – While not a scam, it is a serious credit problem and one that continues to grow. This usually involves a technique called prescreening – or pre-qualification for credit.

    Here's how this happens. Suppose the issuer of a new bankcard wants to find people with perfect credit who also earn at least $50,000 per year. The credit bureau, from their own files can generate a list of potential customers featuring those qualifications. The company can also send its own list to the credit bureau, and the credit bureau can delete non-qualifying names. You may be on this list with neither your knowledge nor consent. Companies can then uncover your financial characteristics without seeing your actual credit report.

    Other examples of irresponsible data collection:

    A company maintains a computerized list of persons who file malpractice suits against doctors and hospitals. This list enables medical personnel to screen out potential "troublemakers".

    A company keeps an index of patients who don't pay their ills, and hotel guests who damage or steal property and don't pay their lodging bills.

    A company that offer landlords "inside information" on tenants.

    These bureaus and services do not notify you when your name is used by a third party. You are thereby denied your right to question the agency and have them reinvestigate. This is illegal because it violates the Fair Credit Report Act (FCRA) a federal law that guarantees individuals the right to examine the information about them on file with a credit report agency. The only way you can discover this is by inspecting your own credit report. If the work "promotional" or letters "prm" appear in the "inquiries" section, it means your file was prescreened. You can request that the credit bureau not include your file in any prescreening program, but presently, the credit bureau is not obligated to honor your request.

A final word on credit scams if you are the victim of a scam, do your best to track down the culprits. This process of tracking down the people should be recorded by you. Keep the time and dates of phone calls made and the people you spoke with, then send this to your creditors. It shows that you are a conscientious person and that you value your good credit standing and that you are responsible. Who knows, maybe you might resolve the issue to your benefit.

If your credit problems are now behind you, your current record of paying your bills must satisfy a lender that you will repay your mortgage on a timely basis. Lenders focus primarily on loan applicants' payment record over the past 24 months. By law, most unfavorable credit information must be eliminated from a borrower's credit file after seven years. A bankruptcy remains on credit reports for up to ten years.

Request a copy of the Federal Trade Commission's (FTC) free publication titled "Building a Better Credit Record" by contacting the Fannie Mae Fulfillment Center at 1-800-471-5554. This publication is available in both English and Spanish. It also can be downloaded from the FTC Web site (www.ftc.gov).

Developing a nontraditional credit history

If you do not have a traditional credit record that shows payments made on credit card purchases, a car loan, or a student loan, you may need to establish a nontraditional credit history. This will not fix a derogatory credit history, but it can supplement or stand in place of insufficient traditional credit sources.

You can help establish a nontraditional credit history by documenting the following types of monthly payments:

- Payment of rent to landlords or property managers; start paying with checks or money orders if you have not done so;

- Payments to utility companies for electricity, gas, water, and telephone services;

- Payments for cable television service;

- Payment of medical, automobile, life, or renter's insurance premiums;
- Local store credit;
- Payment of medical bills; and
- Payment of child care or school tuition.

By documenting the regular and timely payment of such bills, you can help the lender develop a nontraditional credit history. Because these types of payments will not appear on a traditional credit report, you will need to provide proof of payment in the form of canceled checks, receipts, and letters of reference from creditors. Note that insurance or other payments made via payroll deductions do not count in establishing a borrower's credit history.

Fannie Mae requires that lenders request (or compile) a nontraditional credit report if the loan applicant has fewer than three lines of credit on a traditional credit report. If the applicant can provide documentation that includes rental payments made over a period of at least 12 months and at least three other credit references, this is considered a sufficient credit history.

Be sure you understand that nontraditional credit cannot "fix" or replace a negative traditional credit report. Moreover, if any of the nontraditional credit sources reveal a history of late payments, the lender will consider this unfavorably.

Establishing a credit record

If you do not have a traditional credit record and cannot establish a nontraditional credit history, lenders will be unwilling to approve a mortgage. To begin preparing for homeownership, you should begin to establish a credit record. Following are some steps you should take that will demonstrate to a lender that you are capable of meeting your financial obligations:

- Request that all the bills for your housing and other expenses be put in your own name;
- Open your own checking account and pay your bills from this account;
- Borrow money in your own name and repay it;
- Obtain a credit card and use it wisely, paying off the full amount each month; and
- Save all documents that will help establish a credit record, such as bank statements, receipts, and canceled checks.

Taking Responsibility for Your Debt

The overwhelming number of debtors filing bankruptcy are white – reflecting their larger percentage in the population. African Americans are also filing for bankruptcy in large numbers, especially in the middle class. The leading cause of bankruptcy filing is job loss.

All-purpose credit card debt is the most frequently listed debt in bankruptcy filing. Credit card debt is destructive to the black community. Not only do we spend our money on self-gratification items that do not sustain us in any significant manner, we are subject to high interest rates from the credit cards. And unlike the interest from a mortgage debt, credit card interest is not tax deductible.

The high cost of credit card debt is staggering in our community. Suppose Tyrone owes $500 on his credit card, which has an interest rate of 18 percent. If he charges no new purchases and makes the minimum payment of $15 each month, it will take him 47 months (or almost four years) to pay off the $500, and he will have paid $198 in interest. And most people owe a lot more than $500.

Now suppose that Tyrone had decided he could afford to make monthly payments of $35. He would have finished paying off the debt in 17 months (about 1-1/2 years), and he would have paid only $67 in interest - quite a savings!

Eliminating Credit Card Debt

First, for long-term financial health, reduce or eliminate all consumer debt on credit cards and auto loans. This is essential. Borrowing through consumer loans encourages living beyond our means, preventing our ability to save. Interest rates on consumer debt are usually extraordinarily high; and, unlike the interest on a mortgage, the interest on consumer debt is not tax-deductible. There is no relief in the form of tax deductions.

You do not need the help of those fly by night credit repair agencies that you hear advertised on T.V. and radio. These agencies take a percentage of your payment to consolidate your debts. These agencies are doing the same thing you can do free with patience and diligence. Sometimes delinquencies that are removed by these agencies maybe placed back onto your credit report after several months have elapsed. If you do use a credit repair company, inquire if they guarantee their work from current credit fixes, should they show up again on your credit file.

Contact the people whom you owe the most money, and begin a payment plan for each debt. When speaking to a representative of companies to whom you owe money, ask about getting a reduction of the debt, in exchange for a large one-time pay-off. It is worth a try. Collection agencies might prefer to get $500 from a $3,000 debt if they haven't been receiving any amount for the past several years. This means adhering to the budget you designed.

Should you have accessible savings to pay down your consumer debts, use those savings. You're surely paying a higher interest rate on such debt than you're earning from interest on your savings. Plus, interest on your savings is taxable. Just be sure that you have access to sufficient emergency money through family or other means.

If you lack the savings to make your high-cost debts disappear, start by refinancing your high- cost credit card debt onto cards with lower interest rates. Then work at reducing your spending in order to free up cash to pay down these debts as quickly as possible. And, if you've had a tendency to run up credit card balances, consider getting rid of your credit cards and obtaining a Visa or MasterCard debit card. These debit cards look like credit cards and are accepted the same as credit cards by merchants, but they function like checks. When you make a purchase with a debit card, the money is deducted from your checking account within a day or two.

Trim the non-necessities from your budget. Even if you're not a high-income earner, some of the things you spend your money on are non-necessities. Although everyone needs food, shelter, clothing, and health care, people spend a great deal of additional money on luxuries and non-essentials. Even some of what we spend on the necessity categories is partly for luxury.

Purchase products and services that offer value. High quality doesn't have to cost more. In fact, higher-priced products and services are sometimes inferior to lower-cost alternatives.

A good reason to change your spending habits is to purchase a home, but remember you have to be able to continue on these habits for many years, and if you are not confident that you can change to a large degree, then don't plan on it. Accept that this is your life now and consider buying a less expensive home. This doesn't have to be your dream home just your first home. Keep the Dream Alive.

Keeping Your Current Job

African Americans worry about getting and keeping a job at a higher rate than white Americans. This is understandable considering the African American unemployment rate is nearly double that of white Americans. We were, and still are, the first to get fired and the last to get hired, but that does not have to be true for you personally. My father once said, "There are millions of people not working and millions of working people. Be one of the millions working."

The ability to work is one of the most fulfilling aspects of life. Providing oneself with life's necessities through one's own labor is a prerequisite for mental and physical health and happiness.

With an objective look at your work habits, wise planning, and initiative, you can take control of your job destiny.

Take a moment and review your employment history. Pull out your employment letters and other work related information from your Home-in-a-box files. You are using your Home-in-a-box?

What has your employment history been in the past 5 to 10 years? Looking at your past employment you can predict what the next 5 to 10 years will be. Your salary could undergo a dramatic change, or you could relocate to another part of the country but your work habits generally do not change much. If you tend to be employed consistently, then you will most likely continue to be employed. In today's economy, lenders recognize people often change jobs, so a consistent salary is also used to evaluate a person's ability to repay a loan. If you do change jobs frequently that is not necessarily a negative, as long as your salary is consistent. If you have a tendency to go months between jobs or not keep jobs for long, then most likely you will continue this trend. If this is your tendency, then you will have to make some changes, or you may have to re-consider becoming a homeowner, as lenders seldom extend loans to people they consider being employment risks. Once again buying a home is a good thing, but not everything. Losing a home due to failure to pay on time due to constant unemployment will not create value for your life. Some people get along just fine without being homeowners. They focus their energies on other important personal goals and are quite satisfied.

Consider your current occupation. Is your job one that allows advancement? Is your job something that you want to do, or do you find yourself arranging to get fired or quitting? People who dislike their jobs often sabotage themselves into getting fired. It might be better investing in a new career. A career that will allow you to enjoy your work and get paid consistently is the best of all worlds, but sometimes that is not possible to attain immediately. You may have to learn to love where you are at the moment. A phrase I repeat constantly to overcome and transform adverse situations is *Nam myoho renge kyo* (the same phrase from the Tina Turner movie, *What's Love Got To Do With It*). I repeat this phrase in the morning before beginning my day, and in the evening after succeeding over all of my struggles. It can work for you as well.

If you are in a lay-off prone environment or are in a situation, in which you are next up for the unfashionable "pink slip" and the matching "lost my job" shoes, take action immediately. Take responsibility for your job and career by networking right where you are. Author and entrepreneur (and a great human being) Terrie Williams, for whom I published a newsletter several years ago, has an excellent book entitled *The Personal Touch: What you Really Need to Succeed in Today's Fast-Paced Business World*. Utilizing the lessons in this book can help, you, and your career. Make this book a part of your success library. Get your resume updated and using discretion, reach out to every contact that you know in your current company, or anywhere that job opportunities exist.

Be On-Time to Work!

The number one reason people are fired in America is being late to work. Being a late arriver to work is inconsiderate, unprofessional and definitely not in keeping with the wonderful person you are. No matter what your excuse, the kids, sick friend, or the train was late excuses are just that. At least, call your work place as soon as you aware you are running late. Your call allows your co-workers an opportunity to adjust.

One solution to being constantly late: Create a staging area. When celebrities and VIPs need to be somewhere on time, they create a staging area. This is a nearby waiting area in close proximity to where their major event is being held, a place where they can relax and get themselves together. Is there a Starbucks or a bookstore near your work, or any other place where you can relax before you get to work? Within walking distance of your workplace to avoid being held up by traffic, and this place should be inexpensive. Clothing stores are definitely out. Show up at least 20 minutes early to your staging area and have your morning quiet time before you have to show up to work.

Improving Your Working Skills

Evaluate your job skills. Be objective. It is vital that you are at the top of the skills ladder. Improve your work habits and seek feedback from your co-workers and friends. Ask them if they can advise you on what can make you a better employee. Find a mentor in your chosen field, or a life mentor who can guide you through the many ups and downs of a career.

Advice can be painful, but only to your ego, and it can really turn things around for you, especially if you decide to actually incorporate the suggestions provided.

When applying for a loan, your employment history will be checked and double-checked. It is important that your employment dates are consistent with what your tax returns, former and current employers or self-employed documents states. If you have gaps in your employment of 1 year or less, let the banker, know that you took off for school, or to raise a baby, or to take care of your ailing mother. Have someone else read over all of your submitted information for spelling and clarity.

Example of Explanation of Employment Gap for Ida Needa Holmes

During the six months from June 2002 to December 2002, I was unemployed. I was attending PSV College to improve my career opportunity.

After completing the course, I was hired as a receptionist at Titan Telecom with a significant salary increase. If you need further information, I can be contacted at 222 555-3333, between the hours of 9:00 am – 5: 00 pm, Monday thru Friday.

Again, if you have to take a job or several jobs that pay less than that to which you are accustomed, don't let it discourage you too much. Do your best and keep looking for something more in line with your abilities and salary requirements.

A traditional folk saying goes as follow: The lioness crouches backward three steps before she pounces on her prey! You may have to take a step back or two in your career or salary before you can leap forward into a more powerful and rewarding future.

Income from Public Benefits

If you have income in the form of public benefits, there are probably restrictions on how much money you may accumulate and remain eligible for these benefits. For example, SSI recipients are limited to countable assets of $2,000. This makes it difficult for them to show an ability to save money without jeopardizing their benefits.

Increasing Your Borrowing Power

If you have an acceptable credit record but lack borrowing power because of low income or high debt, you may benefit from mortgage products that offer more flexibility. Some housing programs target certain types of borrowers, such as people with disabilities, first-time homebuyers, or people with limited incomes. Others provide certain types of assistance, such as funds for repairs or accessibility modifications. By taking advantage of all the financial assistance you qualify for; you may be able to afford a house that would otherwise be unattainable.

Supplemental Financing

If your qualifying ratios exceed lender guidelines, you may be able to improve your position by obtaining supplemental financing in the form of gifts, grants, or subsidized "seconds" that do not require repayment. This will enable you to reduce the size of the first mortgage, which in turn will lower your ratios. If you have been pre-qualified or pre-approved, you should have a clear idea of how much additional funding you need from alternative financing sources.

Gifts. Gifts from family members, friends, civic groups, or employers may be allowed. Generally, gift givers are required to provide a letter stating the funds are a gift for which they do not expect to be repaid.

Grants. Grants do not need to be repaid and may come from state housing finance agencies, state and local affordable housing programs, state developmental disabilities agencies, endowments for first-time home buyers, Community Block Grant funds, HUD's HOME program, state and local social service agencies, private foundations, and contributions from the seller.

Subsidized second loans. Subsidized second mortgages may be provided by state or local housing agencies, as well as by foundations and nonprofit organizations. They can help make home purchases more affordable by deferring repayment, carrying no or very low interest rates, or forgiving part of the debt each year that the borrower continues to pay off the mortgage. Subsidized loans (called Community Seconds by Fannie Mae) may be used to help pay the down payment, closing costs, or rehabilitation costs that are not covered in the price of the home (see Chapter 5, for more information on these types of mortgages).

Sources of supplemental financing

Following are some funding sources that may be available to low- and moderate-income homebuyers, including those with disabilities and first-time homeowners.

HUD programs. HUD's Community Development Block Grant (CDBG) program provides homeownership grants to qualifying individuals. HOME is another HUD program that provides grants to states and local communities to increase affordable housing opportunities. Assistance may also be available in the form of FHA 203K and Title 1 funds.

State and local housing finance agencies. Housing finance agencies in a number of states have developed strategies to help people become homeowners. By working cooperatively with service providers, these agencies may be able to provide funds to assist in securing the down payment, closing costs, renovation assistance, and low-interest loans.

Community-based organizations. Most communities have nonprofit housing and community development organizations that work to increase the availability of affordable housing to people with low incomes. These organizations can provide information on financing, down payment assistance, and home improvements.

Homeownership readiness checklist

To help you decide whether you are prepared to take the next step along the path to homeownership, complete this checklist:

_____ Do you have steady income?

_____ Are you ready to settle down in one place for the next several years?

_____ Have you completed the asset and debt ratio worksheets so you know how much you can realistically afford to pay for a house?

_____ Have you obtained and reviewed your credit report? Is your credit profile favorable? Have you corrected any erroneous credit references or instances of derogatory credit?

_____ If you don't have an established credit record, can you build a nontraditional credit history by documenting rent, utility, and other monthly payments?

_____ Have you been pre-qualified or pre-approved by a lender so you know how much you can borrow based on your income and existing debt?

_____ If your existing debt will limit your ability to qualify for a mortgage, can you pay down your debt before you attempt to buy a house?

_____ Do you have enough money saved up for the down payment and closing costs? If not, can you enlist the aid of relatives or government or nonprofit agencies that might give or loan you money?

_____ Are you willing to do a lot of hard work and have patience throughout the process of purchasing a home?

If you answered yes to most of these questions, then you may be ready to become a homeowner.

Where we've been

If you have followed the steps outlined in this chapter, you should know whether you are prepared to pursue homeownership at this time. You should have completed the self pre-qualification and approached a lender for pre-qualification or pre-approval for a mortgage. These steps will help you determine the likelihood of your being approved for a loan and the size of loan for which you qualify. You should also be aware of resources that may be available to reduce the size of the mortgage you will require. If these preliminary indicators are positive, you are ready to take the next step toward homeownership.

Affirmation

I accept that I am beautiful, strong, and worthy of self-love. I accept that spending wisely and saving my money increases my feelings of self-worth.

Credit Form Letters

Correcting Your Credit, The Help You Need

The following are form letters that you can use to send to credit agencies or creditors that you have business. Make whatever changes needed to reflect your specific situation before sending. Make sure to keep a copy of the letters that you send. (Be sure to put stamps on your letters, I know one author who forgot and suffered major embarrassment).

Request for a credit report (some States allow for you to receive at least one free report per year)

   Dear Sir or Madam:

   Please send me a copy of my credit report. My name is [First name, Middle Name, Last Name] and my social security numbers is: xxx xx xxxx, my date of birth is [mm,dd,year] and my current address is _____.

   My previous address was _____.

   Enclosed is my check/money order for $xx.xx, as payment for this credit report. Also enclosed is a copy of my driver's license, billing statement, or utility bill with my current address stated for identification. Please send the report to [current address or wherever it needs to be sent].

   Sincerely,

Request for a free credit report based on your credit being denied

Dear Sir or Madam:

Please send me a copy of my credit report as soon as possible. I have been denied credit within the past 60 days by [name of company that denied you credit] based upon a credit report from your company. Enclosed please find a copy of the denial letter.

I am aware that I am entitled to a free report when I have been denied credit based on information you have provided in accordance to the Fair Credit Reporting Act.

My name is [First name, Middle Name, Last Name] and my social security numbers is: xxx xx xxxx, my date of birth is [mm,dd,year] and my current address is _____ .

My previous address was _____ .

Thank you for your immediate attention to this matter.

Sincerely,

Letter of complaint to have inaccurate information removed

Dear Sir or Madam:

I request that the following inaccurate items be immediately investigated and removed from my credit report if found to be inaccurate. These items listed below should not be on my credit report. By the provisions of 15 USC section 1681i of the Fair Credit Reporting Act, I request that these items be re-verified and deleted from my record if found to be in error.

Item No.   Company Name   Company's Account #   Credit Agencies #

In 30 days from the receipt of this letter is the time to re-verify these entries. I will take it as my understanding that failure to do respond within that time constitutes reason to promptly delete the information from my file.

Please contact me when the items have been deleted. You may send an updated copy of my credit report to the below address. I am aware that this service is free of charge according to the provisions of 15 USC section 1681j. Also, please send me the names and addresses of individuals you contacted so I contact them.

My address is _____

Sincerely,

Late payment letter

Dear Sir or Madam:

    I have been made aware that my payments to your account have been labeled "late" on my credit report.

    These late payments were due to....(offer concise and detailed explanation here)

    I have been prompt in paying in the past, and since the late payments occurred for the above reason, please correct the payment history for this account at the following credit bureaus, which carry your account histories: (Name of credit agencies)

    It is important that my credit report reflect the good relations I have with your company. The corrections in the credit report will reflect my excellent financial habits.

Thank you.

Sincerely,

Creditor debt and settlement agreement

Date

Dear Sir or Madam:

I am writing to confirm our agreement regarding the settlement of a debt that I previously owed to your company. The terms we agreed upon were:

I, agree to pay [Company name], the amount of $xx.xx in full satisfaction of all amounts that I owe. I agree to pay the above amount in [#] monthly installments of $xx.xx, without interest. The first payment to begin on [day and date] and each remaining payment on the _____ of each following month. I will mail these payments to your office located at [Company address where bills are to be sent].

If for some reason I do not pay the amount of each payment when due, I will be understand that I am in default of this agreement and you may send me a written notice telling me that if I do not pay the over-due amount by a certain date, the entire unpaid balance will be due within 30 days. This shall take effect after the date on which the notice is delivered or mailed to me.

When I have paid this debt in full, you agree to notify each credit bureau to which you report credit information that I have done so. I would expect that you would respond that any negative credit information be listed as no longer verifiable and should be deleted from my credit report.

If you agree to these terms and conditions, please let me know by signing this Agreement and the copy, and return the documents to me at the address below.

Accepted and Agreed

By: _____

       Company (name of company you owe money to)

       _____

       Name of representative (must have authority)

       _____

       Title of representative

My address is _____

Sincerely,

Request for reasons of credit denial

Dear Sir or Madam:

Recently, your company denied me credit.

I am request a full disclosure of the information disclosed to you by persons other than Consumer Reporting Agencies concerning me. This information must be in sufficient detail to allow me to challenge or dispute its accuracy.

Please take further notice that you are required to render such information to me within 30 days as noted by the Federal Trade.

My name is [First name, Middle name, Last name] my social security number is xxx xx xxxx. My mailing address is _____.

Sincerely,

Chapter 4
A HOUSE IS NOT A HOME, UNTIL YOU BUY IT

"It's pretty hard for the Lord to guide you if you haven't made up your mind which way you want to go."

–Mme C.J. Walker, 1919 – 1967, Entrepreneur

"The goal [was] to establish the presence of people of African descent in every field of endeavor…the problem was when we did integrate Lexington or Scarsdale, we missed what it was like back home."

–Henry Louis Gates Jr., 1950 – Scholar and Critic

Kayla and Marcus had known each other since third grade. Except for calling each other names as children, Marcus and Kayla had seldom argued or disagreed with each other. Getting married and having two children, a boy, Marcus Jr. and a girl, Michele, was their best agreement. Nevertheless, they were not able to agree on a home. Kayla wanted to live in the suburbs. Marcus wanted to be in the city. Months of seeing homes that they could not agree upon left the couple frustrated and angry.

After listening to Kayla and Marcus, I suggested they write down what they absolutely did not want in a home. What I called a "no-way" list. Kayla and Marcus sat down and wrote out what they didn't want for 20 minutes; afterwards they looked at each other's list. Marcus said, "I realize that it wasn't that Kayla didn't want to be near my mother. She absolutely didn't want to be in the city for the children's sake." Kayla added, "I understood that Marcus didn't really care where we lived as long as he didn't have to leave his mother, who lived in the city alone." After that discussion they were able to come together and agree on a home, they had seen a week before. It was big enough to have Marcus' mother move in, and they were able to rent her apartment out for extra income, and best of all the kids had all of the space they needed in their new suburban home. As an extra benefit, Marcus saved hours by not having to spend time driving to his mother's apartment and was able to spend more time with his family.

Finding the right house to make into your home sometimes involves knowing what you don't want as much as what you do.

Where We're Going In This Chapter

By this time, you will have spent a great deal of time planning and thinking about your criteria for the ideal house and neighborhood. Now you are ready to begin serious house hunting, perhaps working with a real estate agent, to find the house that you want to buy. We will go through the process of evaluating houses, making an offer, negotiating the purchase price, and obtaining a property inspection.

With a majority of African Americans living in or near major urban areas with limited housing availability, it is important that when searching for a home you approach this portion of the home buying process with a sense of urgency and diligence. You should be available at any moment to see a possible home. Similar to finding a job you must be clear on what you want and what you absolutely need and go after it full time.

Is There A Home For Me?

Yes, but as was mentioned you have to move with a sense of urgency. There is tremendous competition for homes in most major urban areas. If you are fortunate enough to have many choices, then by all means be selective. Check out as many leads as possible about houses that are for sale. This may include the following:

Word of mouth

You should let your friends, coworkers and acquaintances know that you're in the market for a house. Someone Aunt's best friend is moving back down south and wants to sell but doesn't want to be bothered by all the hassle, sometimes word of mouth can get you in this home.

The Internet

Today the internet is the leading source of property for sell information. This should be your first stop. You can search for home anywhere at anytime without any limitations. Several Web sites show property listings. One of the most popular is www.realtor.com, which is maintained by the National Association of Realtors. You can search by location, property types, and specific features. In the near future AAHBG.com will list properties for sale.

Community and State housing organizations

Contact your state housing authority. They are listed in the yellow pages and the numbers for each state is located in the Appendix. Ask at your local library for community housing organizations.

Banks

It seems strange, but no one mentions going to your local bank. Banks also finance housing construction and would know homes that are available now and in the future.

"For sale" signs

Driving or walking around in search of "for sale" signs may be worthwhile, particularly if you have a good idea of what neighborhood you are interested in. This is a particularly good way to find houses being sold by the owners.

Church

Ask around in your congregation. There are tremendous resources available within the religious community. Ask that a bulletin board be created for posting housing wanted and homes for sale.

Newspaper ads

Classified ads in local newspapers are another good source of leads. "Open houses" also are announced in the real estate section, and you can do some initial shopping and comparative pricing by spending weekend and afternoons looking at houses being shown by real estate sales professionals.

Shoppers' guides

Home finders' directories featuring pictures and brief descriptions of houses currently on the market may be available at supermarkets, convenience stores, and newsstands.

Foreclosure sales

When homeowners fail to pay their mortgage, the lender may foreclose and resell the house in order to recover the unpaid loan amount. Often such homes are sold for a below-market price. You can contact lenders in your area to obtain a list of foreclosed properties. I don't recommend this path due to the legal hassles involved.

Using a real estate sales professional

Although these sources will help you get started, usually the most efficient method of shopping for a house is to consult a real estate agent. It is important that you understand the relationship between a homebuyer and a buyer's broker versus an agent representing a seller, as discussed in chapter 2.

The main benefit a buyer receives from an agent practicing buyer-brokerage is professionalism and a stronger negotiating position. In 1993 U.S. Sprint found that 232, of its relocating employees using a "buyer's broker" paid an average of 91% of a home's listed price, while those that used a traditional agent paid 96% of the list price.

A real estate agent can provide you with an array of services, including the following:

- Help determine how much you can afford to spend on a house;
- Generate computer printouts of houses that meet your specifications;
- Show you houses that meet your requirements;
- Provide information about communities and neighborhoods, including the prices and features of houses in the area, location of schools, property tax rates, unusual building code regulations, and availability of community services;
- Present your purchase offer to the seller; and
- Provide referrals to mortgage lenders, settlement agents, professional home inspectors, and title companies.

A good way to find a real estate agent/buyer's broker is by asking for referrals from people who have recently bought a house. You should try to find an experienced agent or broker who works primarily in the area in which you are interested. The agent should have access to the Multiple Listing Service (MLS), which can be used to generate a computerized list of houses that meet your specific requirements. The MLS printout includes comprehensive information about each house:

- Asking price;
- Year built;

- Number of rooms and size of each room (in square feet);
- Type of siding, windows, roof, foundation, wiring, plumbing, heating system,
- Water supply, and septic system (if applicable);
- Amount of annual property taxes;
- Appliances included with house;
- Date the house will be available for occupancy;
- Lot size; and type of zoning.

The MLS sheet may also include additional comments from the sellers about the neighborhood; special features of the house or lot, newly installed appliances, or recent renovations.

A few tips for working successfully with real estate agents:

- Look at as many houses as possible, but be sure the agent knows the criteria you are trying to match. Provide the agent copies from your wish list file.
- If you feel you are being "steered" by your agent to (or away from) particular neighborhoods, report this to HUD. HUD is in charge of enforcing the Fair Housing Act, which prohibits discrimination on the basis of race, religion, age, and national origin, receipt of public assistance funds, sex, marital status, or disability. You may also want to file a complaint concerning the agent responsible with your local Board of Realtors.

Comparison shopping

Homebuyers typically look at as many as 15 houses before choosing one. I suggest seeing twice or three times as many homes to insure you have seen what is available and affordable. You should also keep looking even after you think you have found the perfect home. The deal on this ideal home might fall through for various reasons and you should have a back up if possible.

You should always have someone you trust from your home dream team accompany you when looking at houses. This person may be more objective and will see features you might otherwise overlook. This person can also help you take notes and remember details about each house.

Comparison shopping is a necessary part of the home-buying process; therefore, you should approach it objectively and consider the following tips.

Keeping records

After you have looked at a number of houses, your memories of each home will begin to blur unless you keep a written or visual record. If possible have your support person or real estate agent take pictures of the house you are viewing; better yet, use a video recorder.

Make a note of your observations about the exterior and interior of each house, including your first impressions.

What to look for

Look critically at each house by asking questions such as these:

- Is the house located in your ideal neighborhood?
- Does it have most of the features you are looking for?
- Will you have access to the types of services you need if you buy this house?

Physical details

Start with what you can see from the outside: the size and age of the house, its general condition and outside upkeep, the lot size, and landscaping. Inside, you may want to make a quick sketch of the floor plan. How many rooms and baths are on each floor? Is there enough storage space? Is the basement finished? Are there built-in appliances? Is the kitchen designed to be a functional workspace? Could the house easily be made accessible? Is there central or room air conditioning? Does the basement flood or the roof leak? Are there water stains on the ceilings or walls? Is the paint or wallpaper in good repair? Does the flooring appear to be in good shape? Do the toilets flush properly? Is the shower in working order? Are the faucets dripping? Is there evidence of pests, such as ant or mouse-traps or other poisons to kill insects?

Construction details

Whether the house is new or old, the quality of the building materials and the craftsmanship, as well as its condition, are important considerations. Is the house well insulated? Are the windows energy efficient? Is the roof in good condition? Does the house appear to be well maintained? Most homebuyers will not be able to answer these questions themselves. Before you purchase a house, you will want to have a qualified home inspector examine the house and give you a detailed report on the condition of the house.

For a fee, a qualified inspector will examine the home you've chosen, from basement to attic. The inspection includes an evaluation of the home's plumbing, electrical work, appliances, the furnace and/or air conditioners, roof and structural stability. Some lenders require a home inspection, and it's a good idea to get one, because it could save you thousands of dollars in future expenses. Knowledge of the house's flaws also may help you negotiate a better price on the house.

Major systems

Are the plumbing, heating and cooling, and electrical systems in good working order? Or does the house need to be rewired and re-plumbed and a new furnace installed? What type of fuel is used for heating, and what is the approximate cost per month and year? How much do utilities cost per month?

Owner financing

Is the current owner's mortgage assumable? If so, is the owner offering to finance the remainder of the purchase price?

Narrowing the field

As you look at houses, you will begin to have a better idea of the types of homes available in various neighborhoods and which areas you prefer. The more houses you look at, the more knowledgeable you will become and the better able you will be to judge whether the asking price is high or low.

When you find a house in your price range that you like, it is important to move quickly as you are competing against many other potential buyers. Nevertheless, do not skip steps, such as the inspection or contract negotiations. No matter how perfect the house may seem, you shouldn't make a snap decision without going back at least once to take a closer, more critical look at the house. This may appear to go against AAHBG guide #4: "If I find the perfect home, I will buy it immediately." But the rule only applies after the house has been checked and double-checked, don't forget guide #9: "I will be patient and persistent and double check everything, or it will cost me!" Visit the neighborhood at different times on different days. Are weekday evenings as quiet as Sunday afternoons? Have you talked with any of your prospective neighbors?

Have others whose opinions you trust look at the house before you decide whether to make an offer. **Never sign papers or put a deposit down on a house without careful consideration** and discussion with your Home Dream Team, spouse and/or co-borrower.

Negotiating The Home Purchase

When you have found a house you want to buy, the next step is to make a purchase offer.

Deciding how much to offer

Most buyers do not offer the full asking price, at least initially. You must know your market. If homes are selling fast, you may get one chance to make an offer, so make it wisely and with a sense of urgency. On the other hand, if you have many homes to choose from, then take the time to evaluate your offer carefully. As you consider how much to offer, you may want to confer with and seek advice from your Home Dream Team. Although the real estate agent that showed you the house will be happy to advise you and guide you through the process of making an offer, you need to remember that the agent's loyalty is to the seller (unless you are using a buyer's agent).

Below are issues you should consider in determining your offering price:

What you can afford

Do not offer more than you can afford to pay. You should know what your total monthly housing costs would be including; the cost of utilities, property taxes, and homeowner's insurance. Do not be tempted to offer more for a house than you can comfortably afford. Guide #4: "If I can't afford it – I won't buy it because I will lose it." has proven to be true more often than you can imagine.

Market value of the house

How does the asking price compare with the market value of the house, based on recent sales of comparable homes in the area? The listing agent should be able to provide a comparative market analysis upon request. You should also check the prices of similar homes that are for sale in the same neighborhood.

Condition of the house

Before making an offer, you should be fairly confident that you are aware of any major problem areas in the house as well as how much it will cost to fix these problems.

Circumstances surrounding the sale

In deciding how much to offer, you should try to determine how anxious the owners are to sell. It is to your advantage to know how long a house has been on the market and whether the asking price has already been reduced. How much did the seller pay for the house, and when? And how much equity does the seller have in the property? (Real estate agents can usually provide this information.)

Financing terms

The terms of the sale may be as important (or more so) than the price. For example, if the seller is offering attractive financing terms, including paying for the title search, the home inspection, and other settlement costs, you may be more willing to accept the price.

Purchase and sales agreement

Once you have settled on an initial offering price, you are ready to submit a "purchase and sale agreement" to the real estate agent. This is a signed offer to purchase the house for a given price under specified terms. You should be sure you understand all the terms of the contract before you sign it and submit the offer. Real estate agents are required by law to deliver all offers to the seller, even if an offer is far below the seller's asking price.

The purchase and sale agreement is a legally binding offer to purchase a property. It should include at least the following:

- Complete legal description of the property;

- Amount of the deposit accompanying the offer, and offering price;

- Size of the intended down payment and how the remainder of the purchase will be financed (including the maximum interest rate you are willing to pay);

- Personal property included. To avoid any misunderstandings or surprises, the contract should list everything that the owner has said will stay with the house or that you want the owner to leave behind. Do not rely on the seller's verbal agreement that specific appliances or personal property are included in the sale;

- Proposed closing date and occupancy date. The contract may include a provision that the seller will pay rent on a daily basis in the event they haven't moved out by the agreed-upon date (usually the closing date);

- Closing costs to be paid by the seller (see Chapter 6 for details);

- Clear title. The contract should state that the purchase is subject to the buyer receiving clear title to the property. Clear title means there are no legal questions as to who owns the property. The title search and title insurance are discussed in Chapter 6;

- All systems in working order. You may want to stipulate that the sellers are responsible for ensuring that the plumbing, heating, mechanical, and electrical systems are in working order at closing;

- Length of time the offer is valid (generally three to five days) and;
- Any contingencies.

Contingencies

In addition to the basic terms of the sale, buyers generally include certain contingencies in the sale and purchase agreement. These are conditions that must be met in order for the contract to take effect. Following are some common contingencies:

Financing terms

The contract should state the purchase price, the amount of the down payment, the total loan amount, and the exact financing terms you will accept, as well as how long you have to find the agreed-upon financing. A financing contingency states that if you are unable to get a loan with the specified terms, the contract will be canceled and your deposit refunded. In turn, the seller may insist that a clause be included requiring you to make a "good-faith effort" to obtain the mortgage.

Appraisal contingency

Mortgage lenders require a professional appraisal of the market value of the property before approving a mortgage. If the appraised value of the house is lower than the agreed-upon purchase price, the lender may deny the loan. An appraisal contingency gives the buyer the right to withdraw their offer or renegotiate the purchase price in this situation.

Satisfactory home inspection

The sales contract should be contingent on a satisfactory report by a professional home inspector. If a major problem with the structure or systems of the house is uncovered, you then have the right not to go ahead with the purchase or to renegotiate the purchase price. The buyer usually pays for the home inspection, whereas the fees for other inspections may be negotiated between the buyer and the seller.

Termite and other inspections

It is standard practice to require the seller to pay for a termite inspection and to require a written certification stating that the property is free of termite infestation and that any damage from past infestation has been repaired. Other inspections that may be included as contingencies include the following:

Water inspection. If the property is not attached to a municipal water supply, the buyers may request a contingency stating that the water must be tested and deemed suitable for drinking.

Radon inspection. Radon is a naturally occurring, odorless gas that can seep into houses and cause health problems. If you have concerns about radon, you can require a radon inspection as a contingency in the contract. For more information about radon in your area, you may want to call the state or county public health department. Or you may contact the U.S. Environmental Protection Agency (EPA) at 1-800-438-4318 or via the Internet at www.epa.gov.

Lead-based paint inspection. For older houses, buyers may want a professional inspection or risk assessment of lead-based paint hazards. A lead paint inspection will indicate what surfaces are coated with lead paint. A risk assessment will identify any lead hazards — such as peeling paint or contaminated dust — and what steps are needed to correct the situation. The sale may be made contingent on this evaluation. For further information about the dangers of lead-based paint, contact the federal lead information hotline at 1-800-LEAD-FYI (1-800532-3394).

Earnest money (deposit)

Homebuyers are usually expected to submit a "good faith" payment with the offer to show the seller that they are serious about buying the house. There is no set amount, and what is customary differs by location. The deposit check should be made out to the real estate firm that is handling the sale, **not to the seller**. The earnest money is deposited in an escrow account to be returned to you if the seller does not accept your offer within a specified number of days. Make sure you understand that you may forfeit this money if the seller accepts your offer and you then decide to back out of the deal.

Negotiating the final purchase price

The seller may respond to your purchase offer in one of three ways: by accepting it, by rejecting it (in which case you must decide whether to make another offer), or by making a counteroffer. If the seller makes a counteroffer, take your time in considering it. You may respond to a counteroffer with another offer — for an amount somewhere between your original offer and the seller's counteroffer.

Generally, the real estate agent presents the buyer's offer to the seller and relays the seller's answer back. The agent continues to act as the liaison between the buyer and seller throughout the negotiating process. Buyers may be expected to put a larger deposit down (again, to be set aside in escrow) once the seller has signed your offer to buy. Be aware you are not required to put down the entire amount of the intended down payment as a deposit.

The Home Inspection

If your purchase offer is accepted, you should have the house inspected by a qualified home inspector. Although the buyer must pay for this inspection (approximately $250 to $400), the resulting peace of mind is well worth the expense.

Finding a qualified inspector

You should try to get a referral for a home inspector from a satisfied homeowner. If necessary, you can find firms listed under "Building Inspection Service" in the Yellow Pages. You should ask for and check references from three recent customers. You can also check that the inspector is a member of the American Society of Home Inspectors (ASHI), a nonprofit organization that sets rigorous standards for its members. ASHI's Standards of Practice are the most widely accepted home inspection guidelines in use today and include all the home's major systems and components.

To obtain the names of local members of ASHI, you may call 1-800-743-2744 or access the Web site at www.ashi.com.

What the inspection includes

The home inspection is not the same as an appraisal. The inspection is meant to evaluate the structural and mechanical condition (not the market value) of the property. The inspector's report is based on observable, unconcealed structural conditions. The inspector will not guarantee or warrant the condition of the home or determine whether it complies with local building codes.

You should accompany the inspector on his or her rounds. You will pick up valuable maintenance tips along the way, have a chance to ask questions, and learn more about the extent of possible problems. You will also be in a better position to understand the inspector's written report.

A pre-purchase home inspection should include an evaluation of at least the following:

- Foundations, Doors and windows, Roof and siding;
- Plumbing and electrical systems;
- Heating, ventilation, and air-conditioning systems;

- Ceilings, walls, and floors;
- Insulation;
- Septic tanks, wells, or sewer lines; and
- Common areas (in the case of a condominium or cooperative).

The home inspection professional should also check for the following environmental hazards (in addition to radon and lead-based paint, which were discussed previously):

Asbestos

Asbestos was used as insulation in homes and businesses for many years before it was found to cause health problems. If the house is more than 20 years old, you may want to hire a qualified professional to inspect the home for asbestos and recommend corrective action, if called for.

Formaldehyde

Formaldehyde is a colorless, gaseous chemical compound that was a common ingredient in the foam used for insulating houses until the early 1980s. It can cause irritation of the eyes, nose, and throat and is suspected of causing cancer. A qualified building inspector can examine the home for formaldehyde emitting materials. Home monitoring kits are also available. For a new home, check with the builder to see whether construction materials containing formaldehyde were used.

Hazardous waste sites

Generally, testing for hazardous waste involves skills and technology not available to the average homeowner or home remodeling contractor. The EPA has identified more than 30,000 potentially contaminated waste sites nationwide. Contact the nearest regional office of the EPA for information on the location and status of hazardous waste sites.

Using the inspection report

An inspection report serves the following purposes:

- Identifies problems before the purchase and prevents unpleasant surprises later;
- Enables buyers to cancel a purchase agreement (and get their deposit refunded) if serious problems are identified;
- May influence the seller to agree to pay for needed repairs, either before the sale or after the sale using escrowed funds; and

- Gives the buyers confidence about going ahead with the purchase.

The inspector's report will not include a recommendation as to whether or not you should buy the house, nor will it evaluate the purchase price. If major flaws are uncovered, the report should give you some idea of what it will cost to repair or replace the problem. You should be warned that a reputable home inspector will never offer to perform the needed repairs and should not refer you to a contractor to perform such repairs.

Home-buying checklist

This checklist will help ensure that you find a suitable house and successfully negotiate the purchase price:

_____ Identify the features you want in your ideal house and neighborhood.

_____ Choose a real estate agent who knows the neighborhood.

_____ Find a house that meets your needs and submit a carefully considered offer.

_____ Include all relevant contingencies in the purchase contract.

_____ Negotiate the final purchase price.

_____ Obtain a home inspection.

Where we've been

We have discussed the process for finding a home and what steps you will be expected to take when negotiating and inspecting the home. Now it's time to prepare for obtaining the mortgage loan or buying your mortgage.

Affirmation

I am becoming wiser and more beautiful each day and my home will be a reflection of this wisdom and beauty.

Chapter 5
BUYING YOUR MORTGAGE

"Sometimes I feel discriminated against, but it does not make me angry. It merely astonishes me. How can any deny themselves the pleasure of my company?"

—Zora Neale Hurston, 1891 – 1960, Writer and Folklorist

"At the bottom of education, at the bottom of politics, even at the bottom of religion, there must be for our race economic independence."

—Booker T. Washington, 1856-1915, Educator

Arnett, a police officer of 13 years, is often able to alleviate a difficult situation with his authoritative presence. Nevertheless, Arnett had experienced anxiety during the mortgage search process. When going to lenders or attending interviews, Arnett would wear his police dress uniform to impress the loan officers. Arnett spoke of his tactics, "I was aware that when I didn't dress in uniform the service was not as professional, although I would bring in the same documents and have all of my information in order. When I wore my uniform, I would get better service and faster responses from the banks. I was determined to use any and every advantage to get the best deal on my mortgage."

Applying for a mortgage is a business activity, big business. You should approach it as such. You may not have a uniform, but you should dress in a professional manner when shopping for a mortgage, or when dealing with others in any part of the home buying process. You have prepared yourself for this moment, and you can be confident that it will still be difficult. You will be successful as long as you are persistent and organized. Failure (giving up rather than re-assessing) is no longer an option for you.

Where We're Going In This Chapter

If you have taken the preparatory steps described in Chapter 3 - that is; if you pre-qualified yourself, or have been pre-approved by a lender, and you have checked the accuracy and completeness of you credit report, you are ready to proceed to buying your mortgage.

Shopping for a mortgage

For most people, buying a home is the largest financial transaction they ever enter into. Shopping for a lender that offers the most attractive loan terms regardless of your real or perceived financial situation is very important. You should expect a range of quoted interest rates, as well as considerable variation in the fees charged by lenders for originating and processing a loan application.

Sources of mortgages

Mortgages may be obtained from a variety of sources, including the following.

Banks and savings and loan (S&L) associations

These financial institutions use the savings or demand deposits (checking accounts) of their depositors to make mortgage loans to home buyers. Some lenders offer favorable mortgage terms to their own account holders.

Mortgage banking companies

These businesses specialize in making real estate loans, or mortgages.

Credit unions

These savings institutions lend funds to their members for consumer purchases, sometimes at below-market interest rates.

State and local housing finance agencies

These agencies, which finance housing for low- and moderate-income people, and usually can be found in the government "blue pages" of the telephone book. Many state housing finance agencies have Web sites that can be accessed via Fannie Mae's consumer Web site at http://www.homepath.com.

Finding a lender

It's important to shop around for a lender because mortgage rates and terms vary greatly, and you may save many thousands of dollars by shopping wisely. To get started, you might ask friends, family members, or coworkers who have recently purchased homes where they obtained their mortgages. Other good sources of leads are the following:

Real estate agents

The real estate agent that helped you find a house may be able to suggest one or more lenders that offer attractive terms.

Local newspapers

The real estate section of many local newspapers includes a weekly comparison of mortgage rates.

Mortgage hotline

To check whether there is a mortgage rate hotline in your area, look in the Yellow Pages under "Mortgages."

The Internet

This is a good source of information for comparing interest rates and fees of a large number of mortgage companies. To get started, check the Fannie Mae Web site (www.fanniemae.com), which includes links to the Web sites of many lenders.

Mortgage brokers

Another option, as discussed in Chapter 2, is to use the services of a mortgage broker who takes a prospective borrower's loan application and shops for the best loan terms available from various lenders around the country. You should find out in advance what type of commission, or fee, you will be charged for this service.

Loan types

Before you begin contacting lenders, you should understand the various types of loans for which you may be eligible.

Conventional loans

Conventional loans are mortgages that are not guaranteed or insured by an agency of the federal government. Lenders generally require borrowers to purchase mortgage insurance (MI), which helps protect the lender (not the borrower) in case of default. Some conventional loans target certain categories of borrowers (such as low-income borrowers).

Seller take-back mortgages

Lenders sometimes allow buyers to assume the seller's existing mortgage. This means the homebuyer takes over the responsibility for paying off the old mortgage. If the interest rate on the seller's mortgage is lower than the current rates, this may be to your advantage. The outstanding balance on the mortgage may be far less than the purchase price of the house. This means the buyer must either come up with a very large down payment or get the owner to finance all or part of the difference. If the owner is willing to finance the difference, the buyers must be able to afford both mortgages unless they are eligible for supplemental financing from government or private sources.

Government-insured loans

The federal government sponsors three programs under which it either guarantees or insures mortgages made by private lenders. If you are eligible, these may be an attractive alternative to conventional financing.

Federal Housing Administration (FHA) loans. FHA-insured loans allow borrowers to purchase a home with a very low down payment (from 3 to 5 percent of the FHA appraisal value or the purchase price, whichever is lower). The maximum amount of an FHA mortgage varies depending on the average cost of housing in the region. For information about FHA-insured loans, you should contact a lender or the local FHA office. Or you can access HUD's Web site at www.hud.gov.

Veterans Administration (VA) loans. VA-guaranteed loans allow qualified veterans to buy a house with no down payment. The qualification guidelines for these loans are less strict than for either FHA or conventional loans. To determine your eligibility for this attractive loan program, you should contact the nearest VA regional office. Or you may access the VA Web site at www.va.gov.

Rural Housing Service (RHS) loans. RHS offers low-interest and market-rate loans with no or very low down payments to low- and moderate-income homebuyers in rural areas and small towns. You should check with the local RHS office or a local lender for eligibility requirements for the Section 502 Guaranteed Rural Housing Loan Program and the Direct Leveraging Loan Program. Or you may access the U.S. Department of Agriculture, Web site at www.usda.gov.

State and local loan programs

Many states and communities sponsor programs to help first-time homebuyers qualify for mortgages. There are also programs designed to help buyers who purchase homes in areas targeted for improvement or revitalization. State and local housing agencies may offer loans with low down payments or low interest rates to targeted buyers such as people with disabilities and low- and moderate-income first-time homebuyers.

Fannie Mae's targeted loan products

By far the largest provider of mortgage financing for African Americans is Fannie Mae. Again, Fannie Mae does not deal directly with the individual private mortgage buyer, but buys the loans that primary lenders make to the public. This allows the lenders to provide more financing. For more information on the following products, visit Fannie Mae's Web site.

Fannie Mae's Community Lending loans

Fannie Mae, in cooperation with local lenders, also offers other loans with flexible terms to low- and moderate-income homebuyers whose income does not exceed the area median income. These loans require a lower-than-normal down payment or lower cash reserves at closing, and most allow qualifying ratios of up to 33/38 percent, thereby lowering a major barrier to homeownership. The principal community lending products are highlighted here (Note: some lenders may call the mortgage options listed below by different names than those listed below):

Fannie 97®. A 3 percent down payment is required from the borrower. Closing costs may be paid by family members, nonprofit groups, or government agencies. The borrower's qualifying ratios may not exceed 28/36 percent for 30-year mortgages or 33/36 percent for 25-year mortgages.

Community 97^{sm}. This mortgage option requires a minimum down payment of just 1 percent or $500, whichever is less, from your own funds. The remainder of the 3 percent toward the mortgage loan can come from other sources, such as those listed above. No cash reserves at closing are required, and a higher percentage of your income can be used to qualify for the loan.

Community 100^{sm}. This mortgage option is ideal for you if you have limited cash resources. Only 1 percent or $500, whichever is less, is required from your own funds towards the mortgage transaction (down payment and/or closing costs). No cash reserves at closing are required, and a higher percentage of your income can be used to qualify for the loan.

Community 100 Plus^{sm}. This mortgage option is ideal for you if you have limited cash resources. Only 1% percent or $500, whichever is less, is required from your own funds towards the mortgage transaction (down payment and/or closing costs). No cash reserves at closing are required, and a higher percentage of your income can be used to qualify for the loan.

Community 2-Family^{sm}. This mortgage option for two-family homes has special affordability features that offer you an opportunity to become a homeowner and a landlord in your community. This mortgage offers higher qualifying ratios and a low down payment of only 5 percent, with 3 percent that must come from your funds, and the other 2 percent that can come from a variety of other sources such as those listed above. A percentage of the rental income you receive may be included in the income used to help you qualify for the loan.

Community 3-4 Family[sm]. The mortgage option for three- and four-family homes requires only a 10 percent down payment, with 5 percent that must come from your own funds, and the other 5 percent that can come from a variety of other sources such as those listed above. A percentage of the rental income you receive may be included in the income used to help you qualify for the loan.

Community Solutions is a suite of flexible mortgage options especially for teachers, police officers, and firefighters. Community Solutions is used with two borrower options. **Teacher A+** for full-time elementary and secondary teachers or administrators; and **Safety 1**[st] for full-time police officers and firefighters. Community Solutions 97, Community Solutions 100, and Community Solutions 2-Family are available under the Community Solutions umbrella – and offer higher qualifying ratios, gifted reserves, a temporary interest rate buy down, and only a 12-month history of on-time rent payments.

Fannie 3/2[sm]. Eligible home buyers must make a 3 percent down payment from their own funds; the remaining 2 percent down payment may come from grants, secured loans, or unsecured loans from nonprofit organizations, public agencies, or employers.

FannieNeighbors®. This program extends the attractive CHBP loan terms to borrowers, regardless of income, who purchase homes in eligible neighborhoods (primarily "central city" areas). For a list of eligible FannieNeighbors areas, access Fannie Mae's Web site at http://www.fanniemae.com or call Fannie Mae's Consumer Resource Center at 1-800-7FANNIE (1-800-732-6643).

Lease-Purchase Mortgage Loans. These mortgages help homebuyers who have insufficient savings for a down payment. A nonprofit organization purchases (and often rehabilitates) homes, which are then leased to prospective homebuyers with an option to buy. The monthly rent payments not only cover the mortgage payment, but also include an extra amount that accumulates funds for a down payment.

Community Land Trust Mortgage Loans. Some communities have formed nonprofit organizations to build or rehabilitate homes on land purchased for this purpose. The houses are then sold as affordable housing to low- and moderate-income households, while the land is leased (rather than sold) to the home buyers. The long-term ground lease includes provisions ensuring that the land underlying the homes is held in trust to serve low- and moderate-income households in perpetuity.

Fannie Mae's HomeChoice loans. HomeChoice loans are available only to low- and moderate-income people who have disabilities or who have family members with disabilities living with them. HomeChoice offers fixed-rate loans with a 15- to 30-year repayment term. A down payment of 5 percent of the sales price (or appraised value, if higher) is required. Depending on income, the borrower's contribution toward the down payment may be as low as $500 or 1-2 percent of the appraised value. To be eligible, the borrowers' income may not exceed the area median income, as defined annually by HUD (except in designated areas with exceptionally high housing costs). To access Fannie Mae's Web site (http://www.fanniemae.com), click on Housing & Community Development. Then select "HUD Median Income Limits."

Timely Payments Rewards^{sm} Mortgages. This mortgage program targets borrowers who have had credit difficulties in the past and would not be eligible for a standard Fannie Mae loan. It allows these buyers to finance their home at an interest rate as much as 2 percent lower than is typically paid for alternative, or sub-prime, financing. After making their mortgage payments on time for 24 consecutive months, borrowers automatically receive a 1 percent reduction in their mortgage rate.

Loanology (loan terms you should know)

Before you begin shopping for a mortgage, you should familiarize yourself with the terms used by lenders. Don't confuse these terms with the use of the word Term when referring to the length of time needed to repay a loan.

Comparing loan terms

Comparing loan terms offered by various lenders can be a confusing process. A Mortgage Shopper's worksheet at the end of this chapter makes it easier to compare lenders' mortgage policies and terms. Basic information about a lender's rates and terms is usually available online, but you may have to talk to individual loan officers for more details.

If you are eligible for a targeted loan with flexible terms, you should begin each "comparison shopping" call by asking whether the lender handles these loans. You should also let the loan officer know that you will be obtaining terms from other lenders for exactly this type of loan.

You should have an understanding of basic mortgage terms and concepts before you begin shopping for the mortgage.

Fixed-rate versus adjustable-rate mortgages

Most loan programs targeting low- and moderate-income homebuyers offer fixed-rate mortgages. Use caution if you are pursuing an adjustable-rate mortgage.

Fixed-rate mortgages. With a fixed-rate mortgage, the interest rate remains the same for the entire repayment term. This means that a borrower's monthly principal and interest payments remain unchanged throughout the life of the loan until the loan is paid off or the house is sold. (The property tax and insurance can and do change over time).

Adjustable-rate mortgages. With an adjustable-rate mortgage, or ARM, the interest rate is adjusted periodically to bring it in line with changing market rates. When interest rates go up, the borrower's mortgage payments go up as well, sometimes significantly. When interest rates go down, your payments may decrease. The method, frequency, and basis for change must be fully disclosed by the lender.

The attraction of ARMs is that they generally offer a lower interest rate initially, which may enable the borrower to qualify for a larger mortgage (and higher-priced house). When interest rates are high, borrowers may also hope the rate they pay will be reduced without having to refinance (that is, pay off the existing mortgage with a new mortgage). You should use caution with all types of adjustable rate (and adjustable-payment) mortgages because they may result in monthly payments that are difficult or impossible for you to manage. In particular, make sure you know how high your monthly payments could possibly go— a so-called "worst-case scenario" – before agreeing to an ARM.

Generally, borrowers should consider an ARM only if they are confident that their income will increase enough in the coming years to comfortably handle any possible increase in payments. If you believe that an ARM is right for you, make sure you understand all the terms, including the adjustment interval, financial index and margin, periodic or lifetime rate caps, and payment caps. (See "ARM loan terms" below).

Interest rate. This rate is the fee charged for borrowing money, stated as a percentage of the outstanding balance. Lenders may change the rates they quote often, even on a daily basis. In addition, lenders will quote different rates for different types of loans. Before making a final decision about a loan, you should make sure that the quoted interest rates are still in effect.

Points. One-time fee charged by lenders to increase the yield on loans. Each point is equal to 1 percent of the amount of the mortgage. For example, if a lender charges one point to originate a $60,000 loan, the borrower pays $600

($600 is 1% of $60,000). Paying extra points at closing can reduce the interest rate for the life of the loan. Points are also tax-deductible.

Annual percentage rate (APR). This is the actual cost of a mortgage after taking into account the interest rate, points, and other costs of financing. Use the APR when comparing mortgage rates as opposed to just the interest rate.

Repayment term. Most mortgages have a repayment term of 15 to 30 years. First time homebuyers usually want the longest repayment term offered because that results in the lowest monthly payment.

Closing costs/fees. The fees imposed at closing (or settlement) may vary substantially among lenders and may be negotiable. You may want to ask specifically about each of the closing costs listed on the worksheet. (For more information on closing costs, see Chapter 6.)

Processing time. The average time required to process and underwrite mortgage applications may vary greatly. Lenders that use automated underwriting, such as Fannie Mae's Desktop Underwriter, may be able to approve a loan very quickly.

Application options. Is a face-to-face meeting between the borrower and the loan officer required? Or can an application be submitted via fax or online?

Down payment requirement. The lender's lowest allowable down payment may vary for different types of loans and may also depend on whether mortgage insurance is required. For special loan products, lenders must allow the more flexible down payment terms set by Fannie Mae.

Mortgage insurance (MI). Lenders may require borrowers to purchase MI to protect the lender against loss in the event the borrower fails to repay the loan. If you have a government backed loan you must obtain Private Mortgage Insurance (PMI). MI enables homebuyers to purchase a home with a lower down payment than would otherwise be acceptable to the lender. The cost of MI is typically $25 to $50 per month.

For conventional loans, you should ask the following questions about MI:

- Will MI be required?
- What is the upfront cost (payable at closing)?
- How much are the monthly premiums?
- When may MI be canceled, and will this be done automatically?

Generally, MI may be canceled when the borrowers have accumulated 20 percent equity in the property (for example, as soon as you owe $80,000 or less on a house that cost $100,000). It is to the borrowers' advantage to cancel their MI as soon as possible in order to reduce their monthly mortgage payment.

Rate lock-in. Borrowers may request a written agreement that guarantees them a specified interest rate. You should ask:

- Will the lender provide a written lock-in agreement?
- Will the lender lock in a rate at the time of application or only upon loan approval?
- Will the lender lock in both the interest rate and the number of points to be paid?
- How long does the lock-in remain in effect?

If rates are rising, borrowers may benefit from locking in the quoted rate as early as possible. The lock-in should last until closing; otherwise, it may need to be renewed.

Prepayment Fee Lenders sometimes impose a fee if the borrower prepays the loan (that is, pays it off before it is due. Predatory lenders commonly use this tactic). Borrowers should ask:

- Is there a prepayment penalty?
- Can borrowers make extra payments without incurring a penalty?

If the borrower can afford to make extra payments or pay more than the monthly payment amount, this can dramatically reduce the overall cost of the loan and allow the mortgage to be paid off early.

Assumability. Will a new borrower be allowed to assume the loan when the current borrower decides to sell the house?

Escrow requirement. Lenders may include property taxes, mortgage insurance, and homeowner's insurance in the borrower's monthly mortgage payment. The lender then holds the amounts collected for taxes and insurance in an escrow account and pays the bills when you come due. If an escrow is required, do the borrowers earn interest on the escrow amount?

Payment options. Normally borrowers make one payment a month, or 12 payments a year. With a biweekly payment plan, smaller payments are automatically deducted from the borrowers' account every other week, or 26 times a year. This may be advantageous for borrowers who get paid on a biweekly basis, especially because biweekly payments result in significantly reduced interest payments over the life of the loan. Automatic deductions may be convenient provided borrowers have sufficient funds in the designated account on each due date.

ARM terms

The remainder of the loan comparison worksheet (and the following terms) apply to ARMs only.

Initial interest rate. Lenders often advertise very low introductory (or "teaser") rates, which result in low monthly payments at the outset and may allow borrowers to qualify for a larger loan. Again, be sure you know what your payments would be if the interest rate increased to the highest allowable rate.

Adjustment interval. How often is the interest rate adjusted? Annually? Biannually?

Financial index. What financial index is used to determine the interest rate? Does the interest rate decrease if the financial index falls? How much has this index changed in the past five years?

Margin. This amount is added to the financial index to determine the mortgage interest rate at each adjustment. (For example, if the financial index is at 7.5 percent on the adjustment date and the margin is 2 percent, the borrower's new interest rate would be 9.5 percent.)

Rate caps. There are two types of rate caps: A periodic cap limits the amount of increase or decrease per adjustment period; a lifetime cap limits the amount the rate can increase over the life of the loan.

Payment cap. A payment cap limits how much the borrower's monthly payments can increase but does not limit the interest rate. As a result, borrowers may end up paying less than the amount of interest owed each month. The result is "negative amortization," in which the homeowner owes more each month as the unpaid interest is added to the loan balance. You should be particularly cautious of ARMs with payment caps.

Convertibility. Some ARMs include a provision allowing conversion to a fixed-rate mortgage at specified times, typically during the first five years of the loan. If an ARM is convertible, you should find out the exact conversion terms and how much it would cost to convert their ARM to a fixed-rate loan.

Applying for a loan

If you gather information about loans systematically, you will notice considerable variation in rates and fees for comparable loans. One lender may  offer the lowest interest rate while another lender charges less in upfront closing costs. Still another lender may have the most favorable lock-in policy. You should identify the terms that are most advantageous to your situation.

Once you have identified a lender that offers the type of mortgage you want at the best terms for you, you should double-check the current interest rate. If the rate has not changed, you should complete a loan application and make an appointment for a loan interview (if required). You can request that the lender mail or fax the application to you, and you should also request a list of documents you must submit (or bring to the interview).

Never sign a document you do not completely understand or that you feel you are being pressured to sign.

The loan application

Most lenders use a standard form called a Universal Residential Loan (URL) application. This form can be downloaded from Fannie Mae's Web site (www.fanniemae.com/singlefamily/doingbusiness/forms/1003.html). Borrowers should be prepared to provide the requested information in the following areas:

- Type of mortgage and terms of loan,
- Property information and purpose of loan,
- Borrower information,
- Employment information,
- Monthly income and combined housing expense information, and
- Assets and liabilities.

It is wise to make a copy and complete the pre-application template and take it with you when applying for loans. It will save time and help you accurately complete the lender's loan application.

Loan interview

A loan interview is a meeting between you and a loan officer from the lending institution. All co-borrowers should attend if possible.

Buying a home is important to a buyer for many reasons. Nevertheless, for a lender, it is a business, as such; you must approach it like a business. As stated earlier, men should wear suits when going on a loan interview, and women should wear business attire. First impressions do make a difference.

Required documentation

Remember to bring the required application fee (which is nonrefundable), along with the following documents, to the loan interview:

- Purchase contract for the house;

- Name and address of your bank, bank account numbers, current account balances, and bank statements for the three most recent months;

- Pay stubs, W-2 forms for the past two years, or other proof of employment and salary for the past two years (if applicable);

- Documentation of all public benefits, such as SSI and SSDI statements;

- Account names, numbers, and balances for mutual funds or retirement accounts, if any;

- Information about debts, including loan and credit card numbers, current balances, and names and addresses of creditors;

- Make, year, and value of each automobile owned;

- Nontraditional credit information, including evidence of rental and utility payments over the past 12 months (if traditional credit information is lacking). If someone else paid rent on your behalf, you should provide documentation from that person or agency explaining how and why that was done;

- Name and address of representative payee, if applicable. The representative payee must provide the lender with copies of the accounting reports submitted to the Social Security Administration for the previous two years.

Rate lock-in

As interest rates are always subject to change, you may want to ask the lender to lock in the current rate while the application is being processed. You should ask when the lock-in begins, how long it lasts, and how much it costs. You should also request a written copy of the lock-in agreement. The lock-in should last until the closing date; if not, an extension may be required.

Estimate of closing costs

Within three days of receiving an application for a home loan, the lender is legally required to provide a "good faith estimate" that itemizes the borrower's settlement (or closing) costs. The lender must also provide the borrower with a copy of the government publication *A Home Buyer's Guide to Settlement Costs*. (This brochure also is available on the Internet at www.hud.gov.) Review this information closely and make sure you understand each charge, or it may cost you.

Loan processing

In determining whether to approve a loan application, lenders look primarily at two things:

- The value of the property being bought (since it serves as collateral for the loan); and

- The borrowers' financial circumstances, including their credit history (because these factors determine the likelihood that the borrower will be able and willing to repay the loan).

The lender will verify the information on the loan application, obtain an appraisal of the property, and review your credit report.

The "four C's" of underwriting

Lenders determine whether to approve a loan by looking at the borrowers' capacity, credit history, capital, and collateral. Be sure you understand the importance of each of these elements (discussed in detail in Chapter 3.).

Capacity

Will the borrowers be able to repay the loan? The lender looks at the borrowers' monthly earnings from employment or other stable sources of income such as public benefits, or a combination of both.

Credit history

Have the borrowers shown evidence of being creditworthy? The lender will look at the loan applicants' past borrowing record to see if they paid their debts and bills on time and if they live within their budget. If you haven't borrowed money in the past, you may be able to construct a nontraditional credit history that documents payment of monthly bills such as rent, utilities, car payments, credit card debt, installment loans, child support payments, or other expenses (as described in Chapter 3).

Capital

Do the borrowers have enough cash for the required down payment and closing costs? In some cases, you may be allowed to supplement your own funds with gifts, grants, or loans from various sources. The lender also will want to know that you will have money left after the purchase (referred to as "reserves") for unexpected emergencies.

Collateral

Will the lender be completely protected if the borrowers fail to repay the loan? The lender wants to know that the property can be sold for at least the amount of the unpaid mortgage. Lenders rely on property appraisals by professional appraisers to confirm the value of the property. If the property requires major renovations, repairs, or rehabilitation, the lender will want to know the homeowner's plans for fixing up the property.

Property appraisal

The lender will arrange for the property to be appraised, a service for which the loan applicant pays. A professional appraiser will judge how much the house is worth based on prices that have been recently paid for similar homes in the same area. An appraisal is required because the lender will not lend more than a certain percentage (typically 95 percent) of the value of the house. This is called the loan-to-value, or LTV, ratio. (i.e, if the home is selling at $60,000 and you borrow $57,000 that is a 95% Loan to Value ratio, because $57,000 is 95% of $60,000.)

If the appraised value of the home is less than the price you have agreed to pay, you may receive a smaller mortgage than you asked for. If this happens, you may have to pay a larger down payment. If you included an appraisal contingency in your contract (as discussed in Chapter 4), you may be able to renegotiate the purchase price.

Automated underwriting

Many lenders today use automated underwriting tools such as Fannie Mae's Desktop Underwriter. This enables mortgage lenders to process loan applications more quickly, efficiently, and objectively. The lender enters information from the borrower's loan application into a computer. From there, it is transmitted electronically to the automated underwriting system, which evaluates the information and makes a recommendation as to whether the loan meets the criteria for approval.

If the loan does not appear to meet the established underwriting criteria, the application is referred back to the lender with advice about areas where additional information might be helpful. The lender considers the recommendation, along with any new information gathered, and makes a final decision. **The lender**, not the automated underwriting tool, always makes the final decision whether to approve or deny a loan application.

Credit scoring

As we discussed in Chapter 3, lenders use credit reports to determine how loan applicants have handled past debts and credit accounts. If you have gathered documentation in support of a nontraditional credit history that reveals good bill-paying habits, the lender should be satisfied.

If the credit report reveals any negative items (such as a history of late payments or failure to repay a loan), the lender may request a written explanation. This is routine practice and not something to be alarmed about. Respond as quickly as possible with an honest statement about what caused the problem and how it was resolved.

Moreover, lenders do not approve or disapprove a loan solely on the basis of the borrowers' credit scores. This is especially true if there are compensating factors not reflected in the credit score or temporary extenuating circumstances (such as an illness that is now past) that resulted in a poor credit history.

Each of the three major credit repositories (Experian, Equifax, and Trans Union) produce FICO scores based on the specific credit information in your own files. Because the credit information is generally not identical, the credit scores may also vary.

What credit scores measure

Credit scores reflect the following factors:

Previous credit performance. The worse the credit performance (reflecting the number of late payments and the length of delinquency), the lower the credit score will be. Also, the more recent the derogatory credit, the greater its negative impact.

Current level of indebtedness. Generally, the higher the percentage of credit use (such as numerous consumer loans and open charge accounts or maxed-out credit cards), the lower the credit score.

Amount of time credit has been in use. Generally, the longer you have had credit and have shown you can successfully manage your debts, the better the credit score. If you have only recently established credit or have only a few credit references, your credit score may be lower than it should be. In this situation, you may be able to supplement your credit record by establishing a nontraditional credit history.

Pursuit of new credit. If you have pursued additional sources of credit, such as new credit cards or an automobile loan, in the 12 months before applying for a loan, your credit score may be lower.

Types of credit available. Although not as important a factor as those mentioned previously, the types of credit you use (such as department store credit cards, bank-issued credit cards, or installment credit accounts with local stores) are also considered.

Credit scores do not reflect any factors addressed by the Equal Credit Opportunity Act (ECOA), including race, sex, religion, national origin, and marital status. The credit score formula does not take into account an individual's income, employment, or residence.

Where to obtain more information

For further information on credit scoring, you may want to access the Web site of Fair, Isaacs and Company at www.fairisaac.com. Under the heading, "Consumer Information" are FAQs on credit scoring, a credit scoring glossary, and other useful data. Links are also provided to credit counseling agencies.

Another useful resource is a booklet titled "What are Credit Scoring and Automated Underwriting?" It is available free, in English or Spanish, from Fannie Mae's Fulfillment Center by calling 1-800-471-5554.

Verification of borrower information

Lenders verify the information on the borrower's loan application by requesting the same information directly from the borrower's employer or other sources listed. This includes information about the borrower's employment and credit history, checking and savings accounts, and rent payment history. If the lender requests additional information during the processing of the loan application, you should respond promptly. It may seem that at times the lender are being overly questioning of you or requesting more documentation unnecessarily, but that is not the case. It is common for lenders to ask for more documentation, in many cases, the lender from whom your lender borrowed the money to give you, is asking for the information.

Approval of mortgage insurer

If the lender requires mortgage insurance, the loan also must meet the underwriting standards of the insurer. If you are applying for a government-insured mortgage (an FHA, VA, or RHS loan), the loan must meet the standards of the insuring agency.

Commitment letter

When the happy day arrives and your loan is approved, you will receive a commitment letter. This is a formal offer from the lender to provide the loan. The applicant is given a set amount of time to accept the loan offer and close the loan. By signing the commitment letter, you accept the terms and conditions of the loan offer.

What to do if your loan is denied

Nationally, African Americans are rejected for mortgage loans at almost twice the rate of white Americans. Although there are instances where these denials are due to bias practices, there are also instances where we have not properly prepared ourselves. Nevertheless, it is important that you do not allow anything in your control to prevent you from achieving your goal. The industry has opened more opportunities for African Americans to get mortgage loans. We have to utilize the opportunity.

If your loan application is rejected, you need to determine why so you can correct any problems or take other action to improve you ability to get a mortgage in the future. You should ask the loan officer if there is anything you can do to strengthen your application. You may be able to work with the lender to correct any problems or improve your ability to get a mortgage in the future. Do not give up at any time in this process. Borrowers with difficult credit and other factors are turned down for reasons that they are unable to correct immediately. But with time, these borrowers have corrected the issues and were approved for loans. Take the action necessary to correct whatever issue is causing the loan denial.

Understanding why the loan was denied

Lenders are required to explain in writing a decision to deny credit. Following are some common reasons a loan may be denied:

Insufficient funds

Are there local programs to help with the down payment? Would family members be willing to help out with the closing costs? Would the seller be willing to finance a second mortgage in order to reduce the amount of down payment money you need? Do any local organizations offer Lease-Purchase Mortgage Loans, in which the prospective homeowner rents a property and part of the monthly rent accrues toward the down payment? If all else fails, start a serious savings plan so you will be in a better position to buy a house in a year or two.

Insufficient income

Are there any compensating factors the lender may have overlooked? For example, the lender may be able to justify higher-than-normal qualifying ratios if your current rent is as high as the proposed mortgage payment.

Too much debt

If you are very close to qualifying, the lender may be willing to reconsider your application, especially if you have an excellent credit history. Otherwise, you may need to pay off some of your debts or choose a less expensive house.

Poor credit rating

If you are refused credit on the basis of a credit bureau report, you are entitled to a free copy of the report from the reporting agency. You may challenge any mistakes in the report and insist that the agency include your comments about any unresolved disputes in its report. If you used a nontraditional credit report to apply for a loan, you may be able to provide additional documentation that shows your bill-paying ability more favorably. Credit is discussed in detail in Chapter 3.

Lenders are under no legal obligation to reveal the credit score on a loan application they deny. You should ask the loan officer to explain any factors that had a negative impact on the credit score. This will help you isolate the problem and know how to strengthen your score.

If your credit history is poor, you should pay off as many debts as possible to improve you credit profile before you look for another house and reapply for a mortgage. Find a local Consumer Credit Counseling Service (CCCS) by calling 1-800-388-2227. These agencies offer assistance in repaying debts – for example, by negotiating with creditors for more affordable repayment terms.

Once you are able to clear up your debts (and learn to stick to a budget, if that is part of the problem), your poor credit history will be repaired, and you may be eligible for a mortgage loan.

Low appraisal value

If your loan application was rejected because the property appraisal was lower than the agreed-upon purchase price, you may be able to renegotiate the purchase price. If the low appraisal reflects needed repairs or structural problems, the seller may agree to fix the problem before the sale of the house. Or the lender may agree to approve the loan if the seller sets aside funds in an escrow account for repairs to be completed after the sale.

If you are denied a mortgage, assess your situation realistically by asking questions such as the following:

- Have you looked into all of the loan possibilities available to you?

- Have you used your home-dream-team to help with research, contacts, referrals, and advice?

- Have you approached more than one lender about applying for a loan?

- Do you have a well-documented credit history, with appropriate recommendations from landlords or others to whom you have made payments?

If you have done your homework and are willing to take advantage of all of the advice and guidance available to you, you may still have an opportunity to own the house of your dreams.

Reporting suspected discrimination

The Equal Credit Opportunity Act and the Fair Housing Act prohibit discrimination against a loan applicant because of sex, race, age, religion, national origin, disability, marital status, or receipt of public assistance.

Women have the right to establish credit in their own name, based on their own credit records and earnings. The lender must count all of a woman's income, including reliable, documented child support and alimony payments (if the loan applicant chooses to disclose them) and wages from part-time employment.

If you suspect that the lender has denied your loan application unfairly (for example, because of your ethnicity, sex, religion or the color of your skin), you should report your grievance to the lender's regulatory agency or to the Housing Discrimination Hotline by calling 1-800 669-9777.

> ## LENDING DISCRIMINATION
>
> **Some banks and lenders have a long history of discriminating against African Americans. The previous problem facing African Americans were the redlining policies that these lenders used to avoid offering loans to qualified persons of African American heritage. Today theses actions have been replaced by more sophisticated policies. The following excerpt from the Coalition for Responsible Lending list the most common activities being practiced by unethical lenders in today's market. The full report dated July 25, 2001 and revised October 25, 2001 can be found on their website (www.responsiblelending.org)**
>
> **The Coalition for Responsible Lending, in this report, quantifies the cost of several predatory lending practices to American homeowners.** Using the best data available to us, we estimate that U.S. borrowers lose $9.1 billion annually to predatory lending practices. For the most part, these practices are entirely legal under existing law; only changes to federal and state laws and regulations will significantly reduce this figure. Further, the magnitude of the problem, we believe, demonstrates that the most important lending issue today is no longer the denial of credit, but rather the terms of credit.
>
> This estimate is based on our analysis of the loan-level components of the following three predatory lending practices:
>
> Equity Stripping—charging borrowers exorbitant fees, which are routinely financed into the loan. These costs result in substantially higher payments while the loan is outstanding and are stripped directly from the equity of the home when a borrower refinances or sells his or her house. At the loan level, equity stripping occurs when borrowers are provided loans that, (1) finance credit insurance, (2) require exorbitant up-front fees, or (3) include prepayment penalties on subprime loans. ·
>
> Rate-Risk Disparities—charging borrowers a higher rate of interest than their credit histories would indicate is justified—often either by the lender's or its affiliate's own underwriting criteria. In fact, one recent study used sophisticated statistical modeling to show that 100 basis points of all subprime lending (and presumably much more for predatory lenders) could not be explained by credit risk.
>
> Excessive Foreclosures—making loans without regard to a borrower's ability to repay. Homeowners struggling to make payments under the combined weight of excessive fees and high interest rates often pay the ultimate price—the loss of their home and all the equity they had accumulated in it. In addition, the equity held by neighboring homeowners is reduced as home values fall in areas of concentrated foreclosure. Finally, there are significant social costs to the pending wholesale loss of neighborhoods of homeowners, particularly in African-American communities [author's emphasis]. While this report discusses foreclosures, it does not attempt to quantify the costs.

Mortgage checklist

This checklist should help ensure that you succeed in finding financing with attractive terms that meet your needs:

_____ Learn about various types and sources of loans.

_____ Become familiar with loan terms.

_____ Shop for a lender offering the most attractive loan terms. Complete the loan application. Arrange for a loan interview.

_____ Gather any required documentation, including evidence of nontraditional credit, if applicable

_____ Do not readily accept what is offered from any financing institution, Negotiate.

Where we've been

This chapter outlines the steps you should follow as you shop for a mortgage loan. We have provided a worksheet to help you compare loan terms. You should not be shy to ask questions, and make sure you understand the answers. When you select a lender, you will complete the loan application and schedule an interview. Once the loan is processed, you will be notified whether your application was approved or denied. If it was not approved, you should find out why and take the necessary steps to correct the situation. If your application was approved, you are well on your way to homeownership. In the next chapter, we will look at the final step: Working the "Closing" and getting the keys to your new house!

Affirmation

As I prepare for being a homeowner, I have permission to be unsure, excited, and at times negative without guilt or blame.

Chapter 6
FINALLY, IT'S MY HOUSE NOW

"Deal with yourself as an individual worthy of respect and make everyone else deal with you the same way."

–Nikki Giovanni, 1943 – , Poet

"A spirit of steadfast determination, exaltation in the face of trials—it is the very soul of our people that has been formed through all the long and weary years of our march toward freedom."

–Paul Robeson, 1898 – 1976, Singer and Activist

Selina was nervous while sitting in her attorney's office. She had never been in a room discussing so much money with so many white people. Selina said, "Everyone looked extremely serious. The whole process was moving so fast." Selina's lawyer was in a heated discussion with the seller's lawyer. The bank's representative was on the phone with the main office, and Selina had already signed 6 documents in 15 places, and the closing wasn't even halfway complete. Selina adds, "I thought I was going to wet my pants. I was that nervous." Then Larry, her support person, arrived. Larry, a homeowner twice before, was all jokes and laughter. Selina said, "I'm not sure if the others in the room knew what to make of him. Larry has supported me in every part of my home buying process. He is my brother and my life saver."

Where We're Going In This Chapter

The closing is the culmination of all of your efforts to buying a home. The details that must be completed before, during, and after the closing are covered in this chapter. If you take care of the details and responsibilities, you should be able to work your closing with little hassle.

In this chapter, the activities that take place in the weeks or days prior to the closing - include selecting a settlement agent, obtaining a title search, and conducting the final "walk-through". Also discussed is what you can expect at the loan closing, the meeting at which the mortgage documents are signed, closing costs are paid, and you receive the keys to your new home.

What to Do Before the "Closing"

As the closing nears, you may be apprehensive that something will go wrong to interfere with the sale. The signed sales contract and loan commitment letter obligate all the parties to complete the transaction. Moreover, should you fail to follow through with the closing, you will lose your deposit and be at risk of a lawsuit.

This is a good time for you to consider who will accompany you to the closing. You will most likely invite a member of your dream team, and anyone you know who has been through one or more closings and who will know what to expect and be able to offer assistance on that day.

Before the date for closing is set, a number of tasks need to be completed.

Setting the closing date

The closing date is scheduled after the loan has been approved and the commitment letter is accepted. Usually the real estate agent will coordinate this date among the buyer, the seller, the lender, and the closing agent. If the interest rate on the mortgage is locked in, you should make sure that closing occurs before the lock-in expires.

Selecting the settlement agent

In various parts of the country, lenders, title insurance companies, escrow companies, real estate brokers, or the attorneys typically conduct closings for the buyer or the seller.

Requesting a title search

Lenders require a title search on the property before closing to ensure that the seller actually owns the property. The title search will also uncover any liens, which are legal claims filed against the property by creditors trying to collect unpaid bills, or by the Internal Revenue Service for nonpayment of taxes. A lien gives creditors the right to collect the money owed them upon sale of the property. The title search protects both the buyer and the lender and is customarily paid for by the buyer.

Purchasing title insurance

As further protection, lenders require homebuyers to purchase title insurance in case a problem with the title is discovered after the property is bought. There are two types of policies: a lender's policy and an owner's policy, which protect the lender and the owner, respectively. Generally, the homebuyer pays a one-time fee for both types of title insurance. Although the owner's policy may be optional, it is important to obtain it. Securing a combined lender's and owner's policy may be less expensive. Purchasing title insurance from the same company that previously insured the title may also result in a savings.

Meeting the conditions of loan approval

Be sure you understand all the conditions of loan approval that were included in the lender's commitment letter. You should discuss any questions with the lender. For example, if the house is in violation of local building codes or zoning regulations, the commitment letter may specify that those problems must be taken care of prior to closing. If the seller has agreed to make the required repairs, you need to make sure the work is completed (and done correctly) before closing.

Purchasing homeowner's insurance

Lenders require borrowers to purchase homeowner's insurance, which protects the homeowner and the lender from loss in the event the house is destroyed, damaged, or burglarized. Typically, the lender requires that the property be insured at its replacement value, which means the insurance company would pay to rebuild or repair the house if it were destroyed.

Shop for a policy that suits your needs, comparing prices from several insurance companies for the same coverage. If you already have some type of insurance policy (such as car insurance), you may be offered a discounted rate for purchasing another type of insurance from the same company. It may make sense to take over the existing insurance policy held by the seller, but it is important to compare prices before making this decision.

The deductible amount is a set amount that the insured pays out of his or her own funds to cover repairs or losses. After the deductible is paid, the insurance company pays the remainder of the costs (up to the amount of coverage selected). The deductible amount can range from zero (in which case, the insurance company pays the entire amount of the claim) to several thousand dollars. If you choose a higher deductible, your premiums will be lower, but you must be prepared to pay any losses up to the deductible amount.

Most homebuyers purchase a standard homeowner's policy that includes the following:

- Coverage against loss resulting from fire, theft, or weather-related damage (such as from hurricanes, floods, or ice storms); and

- Personal liability insurance, which protects homeowners if someone who is injured on their property, sues them.

In addition to the standard coverage, homeowners can buy "riders" that provide added coverage for expensive items such as cameras, stereos, computer equipment, or valuable jewelry.

Lenders usually require that the first year's insurance premium be paid in full at or before closing. They also may require the cost of homeowner's insurance to be included in the borrower's monthly mortgage payments to ensure that the policy remains in effect for the life of the loan. If so, this portion of the borrower's payments is placed in an escrow account from which the loan servicer pays the insurance premiums when they come due each year.

If the insurance premiums will not be collected in an escrow account, you will need to bring an insurance binder (a document from the insurance company stating the amount of coverage and the effective dates) and a receipt with you to the closing.

Obtaining a property survey

The lender may require a survey of the property to verify that the property's boundaries are as described in the purchase and sale agreement. The charge for this service is normally paid by the buyer. The survey, or plot plan, may show that a neighbor's fence extends beyond a boundary line of the property being bought (or vice versa). Occasionally, more serious violations are uncovered that must be cleared up. If the property has been surveyed recently, asking the original surveyor to update the survey may be less expensive than obtaining a new survey.

Obtaining a termite certificate

In some areas of the country, homes must be inspected for termites or other insects before they can be sold. Even if this is not a requirement, it is a good idea to obtain such an inspection. Usually, the seller pays for this. You should obtain a certificate from the termite inspection firm stating that the property is free of both visible termite infestation and termite damage.

Documenting cash reserves

The lender may require borrowers to demonstrate that they have enough money set aside to cover their mortgage payment (principal, interest, taxes, and insurance, or PITI) for one or two months. This reserve, which is sometimes held on the borrowers' behalf in an escrow account, ensures that the borrowers will have sufficient funds to pay their mortgage in the event of a temporary financial setback.

Obtaining commitment letters from agencies

If one or more agencies will be providing funds or other assistance, you will need to obtain a written commitment stating how much money will be allocated on your behalf and how much assistance will be provided and for what length of time. If an agency has agreed to establish an account to cover your long-term maintenance costs, the commitment letter should state how much money will be set aside each month, who will manage the account, and how the funds can be accessed. The lender will require these commitment letters at closing.

Obtaining state certification

If you receive services or funding from an agency, the home you purchase may need to be approved by a state certification agency. For example, the agency that manages your Medicaid funds may need to verify that the property meets the state's housing requirements. You should check with the agency from which you receive funds or assistance to determine the requirements in your area.

Considering automatic payment

You may want to arrange for your bank to automatically withdraw the funds from your checking or savings account to cover your monthly mortgage payment. Electronic funds transfers can be a convenient payment method provided sufficient money is available in your account for automatic withdrawal on the payment due date each month. If funds are unavailable, additional bank charges are incurred.

Considering a homeowner's warranty

If you are buying a new home, you are entitled to a homeowner's warranty that protects against defects. You should receive both the homeowner's warranty and a certificate of occupancy at closing.

In recent years, homeowner's warranties have become available for older homes as well. These warranties serve as an insurance policy to cover major repairs during the first year of ownership. If you are interested in buying such a policy (or accepting a policy provided by the seller), examine it closely to see which systems and appliances are covered and which are excluded.

Conducting a "walk-through"

If you included a final house check, or "walk-through," as a contingency in your purchase and sales agreement, you can inspect the property within 24 hours prior to closing. Generally, the real estate agent accompanies the buyers, and the sellers are not present. This is the buyer's opportunity to make sure the seller has left any furnishings or property (such as appliances, drapes, or a swing set) as agreed upon and that all conditions in the purchase and sales agreement have been met.

If the terms of the sales contract made the seller responsible for ensuring that the plumbing, heating, mechanical, and electrical systems are in working order at the time of the closing, this is your last chance to make sure that everything is working properly. Make a note of anything that has not been taken care of as promised. If any items cannot be corrected before closing, the settlement agent may withhold funds from the seller to cover the cost of the agreed-upon repairs. If you discover major problems or violations of the purchase contract during the house check, you have the right to delay closing until the problems are corrected.

Conducting a house tour with seller

Arrange a house tour with the sellers, either shortly before or after closing. Your goal should be to gather as much information about the house as possible from the seller. You should come prepared with questions and a notepad, or even a tape recorder. You may want to bring along a friend or family member who is knowledgeable about houses to make sure you glean all the information you may want later.

As a starting point, you should ask the sellers to show you the location of each of the following:

- Main cutoff valves for water and gas;
- Emergency switch on the furnace;
- Hot water heater thermostat;
- Main electrical switch;
- Fuse box or circuit breaker box;
- Shutoff valves for outside faucets; and
- Septic tank opening, leach field, and well (if applicable).

One practical idea is to bring labels along so you can label the switches and cutoff valves.

You should ask questions such as these:

- What does the seller know about the history of the house?

- Does the seller have any old photographs of the house that can be reproduced?

- Does the seller have wiring diagrams?

- Does the seller have plans for a renovation that were never completed?

- Who supplies the fuel oil?

- When is trash pick-up day? Recycling day?

- Will the seller provide a list of names and telephone numbers of contractors, electricians, plumbers, roofers, and carpenters who have worked on the house?

- What major repairs or renovations have been done to the house, and when?

- What type of seasonal maintenance did the seller do? Are there trees that require pruning or plants that require special care?

- Does the seller have users' manuals for the appliances or warranties that are still valid?

Obtaining the final estimate of closing costs

In the past, buyers were often surprised with hundreds or even thousands of dollars of unexpected closing costs. Fortunately, that is not the case today. You will know in advance exactly what fees you will be responsible for and the approximate total cost. Lenders are required to give buyers an estimate of closing costs soon after they have applied for a loan (see Chapter 5). Because these estimates are subject to change, buyers may (and should) inspect the HUD-1 Settlement Statement one business day prior to closing. This document itemizes the services provided and lists the charges to the buyer and the seller. The settlement agent who conducts the closing must complete it, and both the buyer and seller must sign it.

Understanding the allocation of closing costs

You should understand each of the closing costs included on the settlement statement. Although local custom varies, generally the buyer and the seller share these costs, and your allocation may be specified in the sales contract. The settlement statement shows which items will be paid from the borrower's funds at closing and which will be paid from the seller's funds.

"Closing Day"

In most areas of the country, the closing is a formal meeting attended by the buyer, the seller, the real estate sales professional, and representatives of the lender and the title company. In some areas, a formal closing is not held. Instead, an escrow agent processes all the paperwork and collects and disburses the required funds. You may want to hire a real estate attorney to advise you and represent your interest at closing, although this is not required in most states. You should be prepared to sign numerous documents, pay the closing costs, and collect the keys to your new house!

Bring any required documents; make sure you have two forms of valid picture identification. A driver's license and passport are acceptable.

Who should attend

You may invite anyone you wish to accompany you to the closing. If you have children who are calm and understanding enough to appreciate this event, bring them. It is important to establish their understanding of the level of responsibility that goes into owning a home. The closing can last up to three hours if certain documents and conditions have not been met.

Explanation of closing documents

The most time-consuming part of the closing process is the explanation and signing of numerous documents. Following is a description of the principal documents that are signed at closing.

Truth-in-Lending Act (TILA) statement

This document, required by federal law, requires mortgage lenders to explain in writing the terms and conditions of a mortgage. The lender must give a copy to a loan applicant within three business days of receiving the loan application.

The TILA statement lists the annual percentage rate (APR), which is the actual interest rate payable on a yearly basis. This rate is higher than the interest rate stated in the mortgage because the APR includes any points, fees, and other costs of credit. The TILA statement also sets forth the other terms of the loan, including the finance charge (the total amount of interest the borrower will pay over the life of the loan), the amount financed, and the total payments required.

If the actual APR varies from the original estimate, the lender must give the borrower a corrected TILA statement by the day of closing. If other items on the TILA statement have changed but the APR is the same, the lender is not required to provide a new TILA statement. You should check with the lender shortly before closing to see if the TILA statement is still accurate.

The note

The mortgage note is essentially an IOU in which the borrower promises to repay the loan at a stated interest rate. It spells out the terms of the loan, including the due date of payments and the location where payments should be sent.

The note also describes any penalties that will be assessed if payments are late. If the borrower fails to make the required payments, sells the house without written consent from the lender, or otherwise violates the terms of the note or mortgage, the borrower may be required to pay back the full amount of the loan before the end of the term.

The deed

The deed is a legal document that transfers and verifies ownership of a property. The seller must bring the deed to the closing, properly signed and notarized.

The mortgage

The mortgage is a legal document that pledges a property to the lender as security for payment of a loan. Although the borrower possesses the property upon closing, the lender has a security interest in the property until the loan is fully repaid.

The mortgage restates the information contained in the note and gives the date of the final scheduled payment. It also states the responsibilities of the borrower to pay principal and interest, taxes, and insurance in a timely manner; to maintain continuous hazard insurance on the property; and to properly maintain the property and not allow it to deteriorate.

The mortgage also states that if the borrower fails to meet these and any other requirements in the mortgage, the lender can demand full payment of the loan balance. In addition, if the borrower does not pay, the lender can foreclose on the property, sell it, and use the funds to pay off the loan, interest, and legal costs of taking back the property. The borrower receives any funds that remain after all these expenses are paid.

Deed of trust

In some areas, a deed of trust is used instead of a mortgage to secure the lender's interest in the property. In this case, a third party (called a trustee) holds the legal title to the property until the loan is fully paid.

Affidavits

At the closing, the borrower may be asked to sign various affidavits required by state law or by the lender. For example, borrowers may have to promise that they plan to live in the house. Borrowers who provide false information may face criminal penalties and run the risk of having the lender accelerate their loan (that is, demand full repayment before the end of the term).

Escrow accounts

If escrow accounts have been set up from which your mortgage payments or maintenance costs will be paid, you should have information regarding these accounts (including who is responsible for maintaining them) with you at closing.

Recording the documents

After all the papers have been signed and the fees paid, the mortgage (or deed of trust) and the deed must be officially recorded at the registry of deeds or the town recording office. This legal transfer of the property usually takes one to two days after closing and confirms the buyer as the official owner. The deed of trust is typically returned to the buyer after it has been recorded.

Store these important documents in a safe place! Place copies in your home-in-a-box. You may want to purchase a small, fireproof safe for your home or rent a bank safe-deposit box.

Getting the house keys!

House keys are the item that sellers most commonly forget to bring to settlement. Make sure you receive keys for all the doors in your new home (including the basement, garage, and gates).

Buyer's Remorse (I Paid How Much?)

If you are like most buyers, you'll experience the feeling that you paid too much for your new home. Buyer's remorse is common and unavoidable. Spending more money on a home than you most likely will on anything else in life gives rise to anxiety and in some cases total hysteria. It's not just you. Everyone experiences it to a lesser or greater degree. Some homebuyers have even been known to back out of a completely good deal because of this condition. The only way to deal with it is to go over the details and facts of your purchase. If you followed the information in this book or listened to the advice of your dream team or a competent real estate agent, the possibilities that you have spent too much for your home is unlikely. You will not suddenly lose the only job you ever held, nor will you suddenly become ill so that you cannot afford to work anymore. These are just fears that we all have.

Buyer's remorse is real, so please be prepared. You can have your friends and family constantly encourage you about the purchase of your home or you can prepare yourself in advance, by carefully going over each aspect of the home buying process in order to verify to yourself that you did the right thing when buying your home.

Pre-Closing Checklist

Review the following checklist as you prepare for the loan closing:

_____ Select a settlement agent.

_____ Make sure all the conditions of the loan offer have been met.

_____ Make sure that any required escrow accounts have been set up.

_____ Request a title search and purchase title insurance.

_____ Obtain a property survey (if required).

_____ Obtain homeowner's (property) insurance.

_____ Obtain a termite certificate.

_____ Obtain probate court approvals (if applicable).

_____ Complete state certifications (if applicable).

_____ Obtain commitment letters (if applicable).

_____ Gather any other documentation required for closing.

_____ Document your cash reserves.

_____ Set the closing date.

_____ Perform the final house check, or "walk-through," with the real estate agent to ensure that all promised repairs have been made and all systems are working.

_____ Decide whom to bring with you to assist at closing.

_____ Review the settlement statement, and make sure you have the funds required for closing.

_____ Request a house tour with the seller.

Where we've been

You will be less anxious as you prepare for loan closing if you know what to expect and what you need to do in preparation. You should have somebody you trust accompany you to the closing, where you will be expected to sign documents, pay your share of the closing costs, and receive the keys to your new home. In the final chapter, we look at some of the joys and responsibilities of homeownership.

Affirmation

I am a joyful homeowner and I will remain a joyful homeowner.

Chapter 7
HOMEOWNING, LIKE YOU LOVE IT

"I leave you love. Love builds. It is positive and helpful. It is more beneficial than hate. Injuries quickly forgotten quickly pass away. Personally and racially, our enemies must be forgiven. Our aim must be to create a world of fellowship and justice where no man's skin color or religion is held against him. "Love thy neighbor" is a precept, which could transform the world if it were universally practiced."

—Mary McLeod Bethune, 1875 – 1955, Educator

"I contend that the Negro is the creative voice in America, is creative America. And it was a happy day in America when the first unhappy slave was landed on its shores. There, in our tortured induction into this land of liberty, we built its most graceful civilization."

—Duke Ellington, 1899 – 1977, Composer and Band Leader

Charlie and Tommie Lee, had the home buying process down tight. They followed the information and advice from real estate professionals, homeowners they knew and attended several of my home buying seminars. They had their paperwork so organized that they were able to advise the banks lawyers during the closing. Which isn't too surprising, as Charlie and Tommie Lee, are both lawyers. Becoming homeowners, they realized that the real work had just begun. They had to reset their priorities. "When we bought the house" says Charlie, " we looked forward too long vacations, dinners out on the town, and relaxing in our new home." Tommie Lee added, "Fortunately we quickly revised our financial and social goals, before spending money on things that wouldn't last. We made managing our finances a priority. Raising three children and a dog, managing the soccer practices, golf lessons and the hundred of other tasks would not have been possible if we hadn't learned to set goals and communicate our feelings openly and honestly." Becoming homeowners has had a amazing effect on the children. Tiffany, their eight year old daughter is smart, beautiful and energetic and speaks with a confidence that belies her years. Anthony, is six and has already has a vocabulary that is several grades above average and is constantly reading when he is not teasing his older sister and playing basketball. The youngest child, Raven who is 2 years old is content to follow her two siblings around the house. Charlie says, "Now we have to manage our expenses like a business, it's difficult but we wouldn't change a single part of it. We love being homeowners. We keep our children involved in our financial matters; of course, only to the level appropriate. But you would be surprised how confident the kids are when relating to money. I also bring the children to the law firm so that they can see the positive side of being responsible for one's own business." Tommie Lee adds, "It hasn't been easy, but over time we have seen the commitment we made to work things out together begin to pay off".

Tommie Lee continues, "We have had our share of surprises; stopped up toilets, pipes that burst, increases in property taxes. We had a house emergency fund, and sometimes we would have to dip into other savings to pay for costly expenses, such as when a storm knocked a tree onto the roof." Charlie adds, "We sit down for at least four hours each month to discuss our financial situation. We take out the receipts for the month and the bills and balance our checking and savings account. We made sure to pay ourselves, by placing money in a separate savings account. We manage our investment accounts carefully. We rely on coupons, Tiffany learned to make her own designer clothes by sewing her name onto her clothing. When we travel on vacation, we stay at hotels that have kitchenettes, so we can save on eating out. We also visit our financial advisor before making any large financial decisions. We kept the same car for eight years, recently we bought a really nice used Lexus. We see some of our neighbors buying the latest cars, and other luxuries and are happy for them, but we know that it was not in our best interest to try to keep up with anyone else. We are going to be successful homeowners for many years. Teaching our children the lessons that will help them succeed and live a joyful life is our priority."

Where We're Going In This Chapter

Becoming a successful homeowner takes even more preparation and effort than being a homebuyer. You have to want it. Your financial responsibilities will have increased, and now you have a home that you must maintain. You need to make your payments on time, and it will seem that you will be spending more money on maintaining your home than expected, but their are tax breaks and other benefits.

Home and Happy

Meeting Your Neighbors

A housewarming party is a great way for you to celebrate with friends, family, and others who helped along the way, as well as to meet your new neighbors. As you settle in and become familiar with every inch of your new house, take time to meet your neighbors. Not only can neighbors be a great source of practical information, getting involved in the community is personally rewarding and fun. Moreover, because neighbors tend to look out for one another and keep an eye on each other's houses, getting to know people in the neighborhood is also a way to help protect your investment.

Getting To Know The House

If you have always lived in rental units, with family members, or in agency run housing, homeownership will bring with it many new responsibilities. You need to learn about the major systems of your house to do routine maintenance and handle emergencies.

Remember to place all of your new housing documentation that you received before and after the closing into your Home-in-a-box file. This file might include warranties, owner's manuals, and other documents obtained from the previous owner, as well as any notes taken during the house tour with the seller. The information in this file can also be used to track repairs, routine maintenance, and home improvements.

Safety tips

The following safety tips may be particularly useful to new homeowners.

Keep handy the telephone number of a friend or family member.

- Ask a neighbor or friend to check on your home while you are moving in. This is a time of change and confusion. Anyone could walk into your home along with the movers, or utilities people, which leads to the next tip;

- Don't allow anyone to come into your home without checking his or her identity. If the cable person is coming for installation, get the name of the person for your area. Have someone else in the home with you at all times.

Emergency Numbers

Post a list of emergency telephone numbers, including the nearest hospital, police station, and fire station, by each telephone. In many areas, 911 is an all-purpose emergency number that connects to the police, fire department, and ambulance. You may also want to post the names and telephone numbers of neighbors, family, friends, or others who can be called in an emergency.

Theft Prevention

Replace all the door locks with new deadbolt locks and have new keys made. There is no way of knowing how many sets of keys there may be to the old locks and who has them. Following are some more tips:

- Lock windows and doors when you are not at home.
- Alert a neighbor if you plan to be away for a few days or more.
- Install a timer so that inside and outside lights come on automatically at dusk.
- Ask a neighbor to collect your mail, or have the post office hold it until your return.
- Discontinue newspaper deliveries while you are away.

Fire Safety

You can help avoid possible disaster by eliminating fire hazards and installing smoke detectors and fire extinguishers.

Smoke detectors. One should be installed outside each bedroom door and in or near the living room. They should be checked at move-in, and retested at least twice a year. Many homeowners do this in the spring and fall when they reset their clocks for daylight savings time.

Fire extinguishers. Every house should have at least one fire extinguisher that is easily accessible from the kitchen and the main living area. In a bigger house, additional extinguishers might be placed in the garage, in the basement, and on each floor.

Fire-prevention inspection. In many communities, fire departments provide free home inspections to point out possible fire hazards such as frayed electrical cords, an overloaded electrical system, flammable materials stored too close to a heat source, or clutter in the basement or attic. Or they may provide videos and written materials to help homeowners do their own inspection.

Fire drills and evacuation plan. Devise an evacuation plan and make sure all members of the household know the safest and fastest way to get out of the house in the event of a fire. If anyone would need physical assistance to get out of the house, the local fire department (and the neighbors) should be aware of this. The evacuation plan should identify a location outside the house where all members of the household will gather while waiting for the fire department to arrive. Periodic fire drills with family members (especially children) and service providers help ensure that everyone knows what to do in case of a fire.

Carbon monoxide detectors. Carbon monoxide (CO) is a colorless, odorless, deadly gas. Because today's energy-efficient, airtight home designs may trap CO-polluted air inside the house, the U.S. Consumer Product Safety Commission recommends installing at least one CO detector near the bedrooms. A second detector located near the home's heating source adds an extra measure of safety.

Storing valuables. All of your homeowner's original documents, including the deed to the house, should be stored in a safe place, such as a fireproof box or a rented bank safe-deposit box. Make copies and keep them in your Home-in-a-box files.

Insurance coverage

Homeowner's Insurance

Insurance coverage is essential to protecting a homeowner's investment, and the lender requires at least minimal coverage. Make sure your homeowner's policy remains up-to-date and provides sufficient coverage. A good way to ensure you always have sufficient coverage is to request an inflation rider, which automatically increases the amount of coverage as the value of the house increases. Also, check with your agent to determine whether standard coverage is sufficient to cover the replacement cost of your personal belongings.

Flood Insurance

Lenders require this if the home is in a federally designated flood area. Even if it is not required, you should consider purchasing coverage if you live in a flood-prone area.

Mortgage Life Insurance

This type of insurance pays the balance of the mortgage if the policyholder dies or, in some cases, becomes disabled. Mortgage life insurance can be expensive and may not make sense for a single homeowner with no dependents.

If you have questions regarding your insurance coverage, you can access the Consumer Insurance Guide on the Internet (www.insure.com). This is an independent site that does not sell insurance and is neither owned nor operated by an insurance company.

Making monthly mortgage payments

The importance of making your mortgage payments on time each month cannot be overemphasized. Buying a home is the biggest investment most people ever make, and no one wants to jeopardize it. Making late payments may result in late charges and damage to your credit rating. Failing to make payments will set in motion even more serious consequences - the lender's action to foreclose and sell the home.

You can guarantee that this will never happen by always making your payments on time. If a problem arises that could keep you from making your payments, you need to immediately discuss your situation with the lender. They may be able to work together with you so that you can keep your house and get back on the right track.

Understanding the loan terms

At the closing, you signed both a mortgage note (a legal IOU to the lender) and the mortgage or deed of trust (the legal document that secures the note and gives the lender a claim against the property if you default on the note's terms).

Payment Terms

Make sure you know;

- When your monthly mortgage payments are due (normally the first day of the month) and;
- Where to send them.

Lenders usually either provide a payment book to help borrowers keep track of their payments or send monthly billing statements. Borrowers are responsible for sending in their payment at the beginning of each month and may be charged a late fee if the payment is received after the 15th of the month. The payment must be received by the date indicated on the mortgage note. Mailing a check on the due date does not satisfy this requirement.

Automatic deductions. Making late payments results in a bad payment record and could hurt your chances of getting an extension of time on a payment in the event of a real emergency. As discussed earlier, if you are worried about making payments on time, one option is to have the mortgage payment automatically deducted from your bank account each month.

Biweekly payment schedule. Borrowers who get paid every two weeks or receive benefit checks twice a month may find it convenient to split their mortgage payment and pay on a biweekly schedule. You should check with the lender to make sure this is acceptable.

Extra payments. All borrowers should understand the positive consequence of paying extra money toward the mortgage (provided this does not result in prepayment penalties). Especially in the early years of the mortgage, most of each monthly payment goes to pay the interest on the loan. Any additional amount is applied directly against the principal. Most borrowers are surprised to learn that even a small additional contribution, made regularly, can significantly shorten the life of the loan.

The Power of Extra Payments

By including a little extra amount with each monthly mortgage payment, borrowers can save a substantial amount of interest over the term of the loan. For example, borrowers who consistently pay an extra $50 per month can typically pay off a 30-year loan in 25 years. If you are in a position to make extra payments regularly, you should ask the lender to calculate the reduction in loan term and resulting savings in interest.

ARM terms

If you have an adjustable-rate mortgage (ARM), the amount of your mortgage payments may change over time. Be sure you understand how frequently the interest rate and payments may change and how the new rate is calculated. Whenever the interest rate or monthly payment changes, you should check carefully to see that the lender has accurately calculated the new payment based on the correct index as of the correct date. If you have any questions about the calculation, you should contact the lender immediately and ask for an explanation. If you are still not satisfied, you should contact the federal regulating agency.

Federal regulators have found that lenders often make mistakes in calculating the new monthly payments on ARMs. Because such a mistake could cost you hundreds or even thousands of dollars over the life of the loan, you need to be vigilant.

Other Loan terms

If you decide to sell your house, can you pay off your loan without being charged a prepayment penalty? In many sub-prime loans there are significant prepayment penalties. Would the buyer be allowed to assume (take over) the existing mortgage? Your mortgage documents should provide the answer to both of these questions.

Servicing issues

Servicing a loan involves collecting and processing the borrowers' mortgage payments and handling the escrow account (including paying the borrowers' property taxes and insurance premiums when due).

Transfer of servicing

Many lenders routinely transfer the responsibility for servicing the loans they originate to another lender or servicer. This is a common practice, and the only drawback for borrowers is that instead of dealing with bank personnel at the local branch where you applied for the loan, you send your payments to another company that may be in a different state. A transfer of servicing does not affect the terms of the mortgage.

If a transfer of servicing occurs, you should receive two letters: one from the original lender and one from the new servicer. **Never send your mortgage payment to a third party unless your current servicer notifies you that your mortgage servicing has been transferred**. If in doubt, you should contact your original lender to verify the transfer.

Escrow adjustments

If your monthly mortgage payment includes escrows for homeowner's insurance and property taxes, this portion of the payment may change if the insurance premium or property tax rates change. The servicer calculates the increase in the monthly escrow and informs borrowers of the adjusted mortgage payment.

You should receive an annual escrow statement from your servicer. Check the accuracy of the calculations and contact the servicer immediately if you don't understand an item on the analysis.

Servicing problems

If you believe that you have been improperly charged a penalty or late fee or if you have other problems or questions relating to the servicing of your loan, you should contact your servicer in writing. Lenders are required to provide written acknowledgment within 20 business days of receiving a written inquiry from a borrower. Within 60 business days, the servicer must either correct the account or determine that it is accurate. The servicer must send the borrower a written notice of the action taken and why.

Cancellation of mortgage insurance

If you have a conventional loan (that is, a loan other than an FHA or VA loan) and you made less than a 20 percent down payment, you are probably paying mortgage insurance, or MI. This type of insurance protects the lender (not the borrower) in the event the borrower defaults on the mortgage. Under the terms of the Homeowners Protection Act of 1998, borrowers with a good payment record have the right to request that MI be canceled when you have paid off 20 percent of the original mortgage balance. For some mortgages, lenders are required to automatically cancel MI when the borrower has 22 percent equity in the property. Loan servicers must inform borrowers about their right to MI cancellation each year.

Even if they are not required to do so, lenders may agree to cancel MI on the request of borrowers who have achieved 20 percent equity in the property. Be aware of this and ask at the appropriate time.

Avoiding Foreclosure Like the Plague

A homeowner's most important financial obligation is the monthly mortgage payment. If borrowers fall behind on their monthly mortgage payments, the lender has the legal right to foreclose on the loan and then sell the property to pay off the loan. You risk losing your home, all the money you have invested in it (including the down payment, closing costs, and all the monthly payments), and your good credit rating. Any legal fees related to the foreclosure may be added to the amount owed. Worse yet, if the value of the property has dropped, the foreclosure sale may not bring a high enough price to cover what is owed on the mortgage. If the lender obtains a deficiency judgment, you could wind up owing the lender money even after you have lost your home!

Planning ahead

The best way to avoid foreclosure is to plan. If you have established an escrow account for long-term maintenance and repairs, you should be prepared when unexpected repairs are needed. Also, you should revise the budget you created earlier and stick to it, as described later in this chapter. If you want to make an improvement or purchase an expensive item for your home, set aside whatever you can afford each month until you have saved enough to pay for the item you want without going into debt.

What to do if financial problems hit

If you start having problems making your monthly mortgage payments, you are in a serious predicament. Even one missed payment can be difficult to make up. If you find yourself in this situation, you need to get help right away. Consider all possible resources by asking questions such as these:

- Is there a relative I might be able to borrow from?
- Can I cut back, at least temporarily, on other expenses?
- Can I work overtime or get a second part-time job?
- Is there a nonprofit or government agency I can turn to for help?

Be warned against the temptation to catch up on a missed mortgage payment by taking out a short-term loan from a loan company or by taking a cash advance on a credit card. The interest rate on consumer credit is very high and will only lead to more serious financial trouble.

Contacting the loan servicer

Many people have a tendency to hide from creditors when they encounter financial problems. This is especially true in the African American community for reasons that in the past might have been justifiable. But this is exactly the wrong thing to do now. If you put off doing anything in hopes that your financial situation will soon improve, you risk losing your home. Instead, you should call your loan servicer immediately to explain why you are unable to make your mortgage payment. You should get the name of the person you talk with and write a follow-up letter that will be placed in your loan file.

The follow-up letter to the lender should include the following information:

- Your name;
- Mortgage loan number;
- Property address;
- Your daytime and evening telephone numbers; and

- A brief explanation of why you are unable to make the mortgage payment.

Servicers are generally willing to work with you provided they believe you are acting in good faith (that is, you sincerely want to make your monthly mortgage payments and keep your home) and it appears the problem can be resolved. The servicer is more apt to be sympathetic if your payment history is good and you contact the servicer right away, rather than waiting for the servicer to initiate action.

Do not avoid telephone calls from your servicer if you are behind in making payments. You should also not make repayment promises you know you won't be able to keep.

Working with a credit counselor

If the lender thinks there is a good chance that you can bring your payments up to date, they may suggest a credit counselor. The counselor may either work for the lender or for an independent credit counseling agency. Credit counselors are trained to give advice and help homeowners who are having trouble paying their bills manage their money better. They can help you develop a realistic household budget and set up a repayment plan that will allow you to get back on track with your mortgage payments.

- To locate a housing counseling agency in your community, call 1-800-388-2227.

- Or contact Fannie Mae's Consumer Resource Center at 1-800-7FANNIE (1-800-7326643).

Alternatives to foreclosure

Depending on your situation and the type of mortgage you have, the lender might offer some type of temporary or permanent assistance. If you have an FHA or VA mortgage, the loan servicer must follow the foreclosure policies set by HUD or VA, respectively. If Fannie Mae has purchased your loan, the servicer may discuss various options, depending on whether the borrowers can afford to keep the home. To find out if Fannie Mae owns a loan, you may contact the Consumer Resource Center at 1-800-7FANNIE (1-800-732-6643) and provide your property address. Fannie Mae can check to see whether that property is in their database.

If you can afford to keep your home

Sometimes you may experience a temporary reduction in income or a financial hardship, such as an illness. When this happens you may temporarily be unable to afford your mortgage payments. Once the situation improves, you are then able to resume your scheduled mortgage payments. By working cooperatively with the lender, you may be able to catch up on your mortgage obligations and salvage your credit record.

If the borrower is experiencing a temporary financial setback, the servicer may suggest one of the following options:

Repayment plan. The servicer arranges for you to make an additional payment each month (in addition to the regular mortgage payment) until the loan becomes current.

Forbearance. This is a formal written agreement under which a lender agrees to reduce or suspend your monthly payments for a specific period. After the agreed-upon period, you resume your regular payments and pay an additional amount each month to make up for the missed payments.

Loan modification. In extreme cases, the lender may be willing to change the terms of a your mortgage (for example, by lowering the interest rate, changing an adjustable-rate mortgage to a fixed rate, or increasing the repayment period) in order to reduce your monthly payments and prevent foreclosure.

If you cannot afford to keep your home

When you experience financial hardships from which you cannot recover, the following options may be available to help avoid foreclosure:

Loan assumption. This is a method of transferring ownership of a home to a new buyer who agrees to take responsibility for the existing mortgage. Not all mortgages are assumable, so this option must first be discussed with the servicer.

Pre-foreclosure sale. The servicer (and the investor, such as Fannie Mae, if any) allows the property to be sold and agrees to accept the proceeds of the sale in satisfaction of the mortgage loan even though the sale may yield less than the amount owed on the mortgage.

Deed in lieu of foreclosure. Under this option, the borrower voluntarily gives the property deed to the servicer in satisfaction of the mortgage loan. Generally, this is a last alternative to foreclosure.

Beware of dishonest "buyers"

Unfortunately, some individuals and companies try to take advantage of homeowners who are having financial difficulties. Many homeowners have been cheated by individuals who say they can help but actually cause the homeowner to lose everything. These "distressed homeowner" programs may look enticing to people who can no longer make their monthly mortgage payments. If you believe the only way out of your financial difficulty is to sell the house, you should talk with and seek advice from your lender, credit counselor, dream team, or a real estate attorney before signing any form or sales agreement.

Getting help

As always, ask the members of your dream team for advice or help. If you run into problems, many real estate agents are willing to answer questions or direct you to an appropriate agency after the sale. For more information or for assistance with any homeownership issue, contact the agencies listed in additional resources in the appendix.

Maintaining the home

Often, only after settling in does reality hit the new homeowner. Unless they have bought into a condominium or cooperative, homeowners must take responsibility for many chores they may have taken for granted as tenants, for example, mowing the lawn, raking leaves, shoveling snow, and cleaning gutters. Gone are the days of phoning the landlord or building maintenance staff to report a leak or faulty outlet. Make sure you are prepared to deal with this new reality.

Here are some suggestions that may help ease the transition.

Preventive maintenance

In many cases, preventive maintenance can actually extend the life of things and avoid the need for expensive repairs. For this reason, you would be wise to create a seasonal checklist and mark the calendar at the beginning of each year to highlight upcoming chores. Once you have established a routine, these chores won't take long and are well worth the effort.

Reviewing the home inspection report you received before you bought the house will help identify specific areas needing attention.

Energy conservation measures

Many new homeowners are shocked to discover the high cost of utilities. When you see your first heating or air-conditioning bills, you may be eager to find ways to conserve energy. Many low-cost ways to improve the energy efficiency of a home don't require specialized skills. Ask the following questions:

- Does the house need more or better insulation?
- Are storm windows installed in each window?
- Is weather stripping or caulking needed?
- Is the attic properly ventilated?
- Is the room temperature regulated by a timed (programmable) thermostat?

The local utility company or state conservation agency may provide energy-saving tips specific to your geographic area. Most electric companies will do a free home inspection to help homeowners find ways to reduce their consumption of electricity. Free weatherization services may be available to low-income homeowners. Investigate federal tax rebates and utility company incentives, including low-interest loans, for installing energy-efficient heating and cooling systems.

Of course, conserving energy is not a one-time effort. Homeowners must continue to monitor their use of utilities and carry out maintenance projects aimed at cutting energy bills each year.

The U.S. Department of Energy and the Environmental Protection Agency jointly sponsor the Home Energy Saver, a Web-based tool to help homeowners identify the best ways to save energy in their homes and find the resources to accomplish the energy-saving measures. The Web site is located at http://hes.lbl.gov.

Do-it-yourself repairs

Doing routine maintenance and making small repairs before issues, turn into big projects can save both money and aggravation. Moreover, many basic home repairs don't require expensive tools or a lot of experience. Get your family, friends, and neighbors for hands-on help or advice with small projects such as painting the exterior woodwork, building a deck, or installing an air conditioner.

Homeowners should have at least the following basic tools to get started:

- Hammer and an assortment of nails,
- Straight-blade and Phillips (or combination) screwdrivers,

- Slip-joint pliers,
- Handsaw,
- Wall scraper,
- Tape measure,
- Flashlight,
- Plunger (one that works for both sinks and toilets), and
- A stepladder.

Basic home repair courses are offered by many community colleges and cooperative extension service offices, as well as by local hardware stores and building suppliers. Public libraries and local bookstores may have basic home maintenance books or videos on maintenance and repairs. And if you have access to the Internet, dozens of Web sites are devoted to home maintenance and repair topics.

Home improvements

If your new home requires improvement or other major repairs, you need to take the time to prepare financially. If the improvements are not urgent, consider postponing any major renovations for a year or so to make sure you can comfortably afford your mortgage payments and routine maintenance expenses.

When you need to hire an expert, the following tips may help get the project done right for a fair price.

Hiring a qualified contractor

You should attempt to locate a person who has expertise in your area and who is willing to be flexible and creative when it comes to ensuring that your home is tailored to your specific needs.

Requesting referrals. To find a qualified contractor, look for companies that work in the area and have a reputation for high-quality work. You may receive more personalized service and a better price from an individual than from a big company. Ask for recommendations from people who have made similar modifications to their homes and have received good service.

Checking references. You should get the names and telephone numbers of a contractor's previous customers and call them to find out if they were satisfied with the contractor's work. If a contractor comes to your door trying to sell his or her services, you should be suspicious. Reliable contractors do not usually operate this way.

Obtaining a written contract. Ideally, homeowners should get written estimates from at least three contractors who are qualified to complete the required work. The more precise the specifications the homeowners provide, the more realistic the bids will be. Compare the estimates, including the details of how and when the work will be completed, to determine which contractor is offering the best price.

Make sure you find out whether the quoted price is an estimate or a firm bid. A bid is an offer from the contractor specifying that the work will be completed for the stated cost. With an estimate, the contractor has the right to charge more for the work, depending on how long it takes or how complex the job becomes. Often, especially with older houses, contractors will not give a firm bid because it's impossible to know until they start the work what they'll find and how hard it will be to fix.

Get a written contract. For major construction projects, insist on a written contract from the contractor. The contract should specify exactly what work is to be performed, start and completion dates, and a schedule of payments. Always withhold part of the payment until the entire job is completed to your satisfaction.

Financing major repairs and home improvements

No matter how well you plan and budget, at some point you may be faced with costly emergency repairs you can't afford. The following are some suggestions in such cases:

Public or private repair programs. There may be a state or local government program or a nonprofit agency in your area that will help pay for needed repairs. Many communities also have volunteer organizations and community housing programs that provide assistance with repairs.

Warranties and insurance coverage. Check whether the item needing repair (for example, the heating system or washing machine) is covered by a warranty. Some repairs (such as those necessitated by water damage) may be covered by your homeowner's insurance policy. For condominium owners, damage to common areas may be covered by the association's insurance policy.

Home improvement and personal loans. Home improvement loans may be a source of funds, especially for homeowners who have little or no equity in the property. Personal loans from a bank or credit union may be another option. Or you may find a contractor who will provide financing. Fannie Mae offers

HomeStyle ® second mortgages that provide funds to repair, remodel, or enlarge a home. Another possibility is the FHA Title I Home Improvement Loan.

Home equity loans. Home equity loans enable homeowners to borrow against the equity they have built up in the home. They may either borrow a fixed amount that is repayable in equal monthly installments or a line of credit that allows the homeowner to borrow money, as it is needed. An advantage of home equity loans is that the interest paid may be deductible. A disadvantage is that the borrowers are putting their house up as collateral, which means they risk losing their home in the event they are unable to repay the loan.

Be sure you understand the terms of the loan and how it is to be repaid. Shop around for the lowest interest rate, just as you did for your mortgage. You also need to know whether the loan is repayable in monthly installments or whether you must repay it all at once.

Household budgeting

As a new homeowner, you may feel the need to buy many things - perhaps a new lawn mower, an air conditioner, or some new furniture. Try to wait a few months, if possible, until you are confident that you can handle your new mortgage payments. Although mortgage payments should be your top financial priority, you also can't afford to get behind on your utility bills or your car payments. This leads to the important subject of prioritizing expenses and managing a household budget.

Creating a budget

Most people would like to spend less and save more, but you just don't know where to start. For many of us, creating a budget is like starting a diet - well, there's always tomorrow. Do not to delay. Take that first step today!

A budget doesn't have to be complicated. It's simply a picture of the money flowing in (income) and the money flowing out (expenses) of the household. The goal is to ensure that money is flowing in faster than it's flowing out. The process of developing a budget will help you set goals and priorities as well as keep track of how you spend your money. A budget will also help you identify poor spending habits before they cause problems. The budget worksheet that you completed in Chapter 3 is a good basis from which to develop a budget.

The basic steps to developing and managing a budget are the following: (1) determine the household's total net income; (2) determine the household's total monthly expenses; (3) compare monthly expenses with monthly income; (4) analyze where to cut back; and (5) set goals.

Step 1: Determining total net income

For budget purposes, you need to know the total amount of money received each month. This includes your benefits, take-home or net pay (that is, after deductions for taxes, medical insurance, and so on), and any other regular income you receive. Review and update the income figures in your budget worksheet.

To calculate monthly income:

- If paid weekly, multiply take-home pay by 52 and divide by 12.

- If paid every other week, multiply take-home pay by two.

Annual bonuses, gifts, income tax refunds, occasional overtime, and other infrequent sources of income should not be included. You should focus on what you receive on a regular basis each month.

Step 2: Determining total monthly expenses

Review and update the "proposed" expense figures in your budget worksheet.

Housing costs. These figures should reflect your actual mortgage payments (including property taxes and property insurance) and your average monthly utility costs (gas, electricity, water and sewage, trash collection, cable television, and telephone) and homeowner's association or condo fees, if applicable. Any annual, semi-annual, and quarterly expenses should be broken down into a monthly figure. For example, if a car insurance premium of $150 comes due twice a year, you should set aside $25 each month to meet this expense.

Using a Budget Calendar. Use a calendar to note the due date of all your monthly expenses (mortgage, utilities, car payments, etc.). Pay particular attention to expenses that come due quarterly or annually, such as property taxes, property insurance, and car insurance and registration. A budget calendar will ensure that you have set aside money to cover these expenses.

Home maintenance allowance. Homeowners need to budget for regular home maintenance and emergency repairs. Some financial advisers suggest saving 1 percent of the purchase price of the house for annual maintenance and repairs. This means that if you paid $80,000 for your house, you should set aside $800 per year (or $65 per month). This amount should be adjusted as appropriate for each individual situation. Your maintenance costs may be higher if you have an older house with the original plumbing, wiring, furnace, and roof.

Other monthly debt payments. For budget purposes, don't include any expenses (such as income taxes and health insurance) that are deducted from your paycheck. Include all other regular debt payments such as credit cards and car loans.

Credit card debt. If you have credit card debt, you should pay it off as quickly as possible. Because credit card companies usually require only a minimum payment each month, many consumers are tempted to pay only this minimum amount. This is a serious mistake because it may take years to pay off even a small credit card balance at this rate.

Because the interest rate on credit cards is so high, you should have a definite plan for paying off this debt as quickly as possible. You might use the following strategies:

- Compare the terms of multiple cards, including the annual percentage rate (APR), finance charge, annual fee (if any), credit limit, grace period (the number of days after the due date before a penalty is charged), and minimum monthly payment. Combine existing credit card debt under the card that offers the lowest APR.

- Use only one or two credit cards consistently, and pay for all new purchases when they are billed each month.

- Close out all unused credit card accounts by contacting the bank that issued the cards. (Simply cutting up the plastic will not remove the account from the cardholder's credit report.)

- Resist the temptation to sign up for "preapproved" credit card, offers. Shred these offers and throw them away!

Cash purchases. Most people find it hard to keep track of their cash expenditures. They have a record of payments made by check and credit card, but they often have no idea how much they and their family members spend for entertainment or miscellaneous cash expenditures. Begin "guess-timating" these expenses, and then verify their accuracy by tracking out-of-pocket expenditures for a two-month period. You may be surprised at how those little impulse purchases add up!

Emergency reserve fund. No homeowner can afford to be without a serious savings plan. Everyone needs a safety net to fall back on. Many financial advisers suggest saving 5 percent of take-home pay in a separate account that is set aside only for a real emergency. The goal should be to build up a reserve equal to three to six months' worth of expenses. Most people find if they simply save whatever is left at the end of each pay period; they wind up with no savings at all. Establishing an emergency reserve fund should be a high priority. Failure to put aside money for an emergency can mean losing your home in the event of a temporary financial setback.

Step 3: Comparing expenses with income

If your net income covers your monthly expenses, skip to step five, setting goals. If your expenses exceed net income, you are in trouble! You can't keep this up for long before you will face a real financial crisis. If your finances look fine on paper but you often run out of money before the end of each pay period, that's also a sign of trouble.

If the "buy now, pay later" way of life has left you with a mounting pile of bills, you could be headed for real trouble. If you're in over your head, get help. Contact Fannie Mae's Hotline at 1-8007FANNIE (1-800-732-6643) to find a free consumer credit counseling agency in your community. Or check Fannie Mae's consumer Web site at http://www.homepath.com.

Step 4: Deciding where to cut back

Cutting back on your spending!

First, categorize your monthly expenses as either fixed or discretionary expenses. Fixed expenses, such as the mortgage payment, utilities, and insurance premiums, are obligations that cannot be changed. Discretionary expenses are those over which you have control, such as entertainment, eating out, and clothing.

Second, categorize your discretionary expenses as either needs or wants. Food and clothing are necessary expenses, but the amount spent on these items is partly discretionary. For example, you might be able to decrease your food budget by taking a lunch to work rather than always eating out. Or you might decide you don't really need another new pair of shoes.

Third, prioritize your "wants." Decide how much you can really afford to pay for items in this last list. Save on entertainment expenses (such as getting books out of the local public library rather than buying them, renting a movie rather than going to the movie theater, and going to free concerts and events). This will help create a realistic spending (and savings!) plan that will allow you to live within your budget.

Step 5: Setting financial goals

If you have enough income to cover all your expenses (and you have home maintenance and emergency funds and are paying down your credit card debt at a reasonable rate), congratulations! You can now begin to establish some short-term goals (perhaps a home improvement project, a new stereo, a car, or a vacation) and long-term goals (such as saving for retirement). Decide how much you would need to save each month to achieve one or more of your goals, and put this money aside in a separate bank account.

Keep in mind; however, that recipients of government benefits may be limited as to the amount they can save without jeopardizing their benefits or eligibility for Medicaid.

Automated Teller Machines (ATMs)
By making it so easy to withdraw cash, ATMs are some people's worst enemy. Some people find that cash "eats a hole in their pocket." If they have it, they spend it. In addition, many banks charge fees for the use of ATMs or allow only two or three withdrawals a month before imposing a fee. In some cases, ATM users are charged twice - by their own bank and by the bank operating the ATM machine.

Living within one's budget

Creating a budget can help put you on the road to greater financial security. But you won't reach your goal unless you actually use your budget on a consistent basis. A budget is not something that can be created and then put aside and forgotten. Look at your budget at least once a month (perhaps when paying bills) to see how you are doing. If you continue to spend more than you're bringing in, you need to keep looking for ways to cut back. You can't afford to give up!

The following budget tips may prove helpful:

- Be a wise grocery shopper. Try not to go food shopping when you're hungry. Always use a grocery list so you only buy items you need. Compare prices of similar products and of the same product in different size packages. Use coupons to reduce your grocery bill but only to buy items you need. Remember to compare prices.

- Plan for major purchases rather than making impulsive decisions. Whenever you charge anything, look carefully at the financing terms. Often the retailers that offer the easiest terms (such as no payments due for three months) charge the highest rates. Shop around and compare. Try to save up for things you need, rather than charging them. You'll pay less, and while you are saving, you may decide that you'd rather use the money for something else.

- Most people find that credit cards create a temptation to spend money they don't have. Establish the habit of using checks to make purchases and pay bills, rather than using a credit card. Store-issued credit cards usually have higher interest rates than bank-issued cards (such as Visa or MasterCard).

- Sign up for your gas and electric companies' "budget" or "average payment" plan. The company determines an estimated cost per year based on your past consumption, then divides this figure by 12. You pay this amount monthly, no matter how much gas or electricity you actually use. Once a year, the utility adjusts the monthly payment up or down to reflect actual usage. Paying a set amount each month helps with budgeting because it spreads the high cost of winter heating throughout the year.

Financial benefits of homeownership

Along with the increased responsibilities that come with homeownership, remember there are many financial benefits of owning your own home.

Tax benefits

For many years, the federal government has promoted homeownership by providing homeowners with significant tax benefits that are not available to renters. A rundown of these benefits follow. To take advantage of these deductions, taxpayers must use IRS Form 1040 rather than Form 1040EZ.

Interest deduction

The interest paid on a home mortgage is deductible, which can save homeowners a lot of money, especially in the early years of a mortgage when most of a borrower's monthly mortgage payment is interest.

Example. Suppose you are paying 8 percent interest on an $80,000 fixed-rate mortgage payable over 30 years. The monthly payments (principal and interest only) are $587.02, or $7,044 per year. In the first year of the loan, you will pay $6,375.86 in interest and only $668.26 in principal. The entire interest amount is a deductible expense.

The interest paid on a second mortgage is also deductible. Moreover, in the first year, homebuyers can deduct any points that they (or the seller) paid to the lender in the process of obtaining the mortgage.

Property tax deduction

Property taxes paid to local jurisdictions are deductible, and some states allow deductions for these taxes. You may also qualify for local property tax rebates offered to low- and moderate-income or first-time homeowners.

Depreciation of rental income

Homeowners who rent out part of their home must pay taxes on the rental income. They can first deduct the cost of repairs, operating expenses (including utilities, insurance, and advertising for tenants), and an annual depreciation allowance.

Capital gains exclusion

Generally, when people sell something for more than they paid for it, they must pay a capital gains tax. Again, homeowners receive preferential treatment in this regard. Homeowners who sell a property in which they have lived for at least two of the past five years are not taxed on up to $250,000 of profit (or $500,000 for a husband and wife who file a joint income tax return).

For tax purposes, it's important to keep accurate and complete records of the cost of any home improvements. Although these expenditures are not deductible, they increase the home's "basis," which in turn determines the amount of the gain for tax purposes. Even the closing costs paid by the borrower can increase the home's basis. Keep the HUD-1 Settlement Statement in a safe place, preferably your Home-in-a-box with your other important papers.

Using homeowner's equity

Owning a home is an investment. As borrowers pay down their mortgage, they build up equity (their ownership interest) in their home. In addition, if the market value of the house increases, your equity increases. You can quickly calculate equity as follows:

Current value of house - Mortgage balance = Equity.

For example if your home is worth $80,000 right now and you have $55,000 left to pay on your mortgage, you have $25,000 in equity.

Homeowners can take advantage of this equity buildup in a number of ways.

Second mortgages

One way to take advantage of the equity buildup in a home is to take out a second mortgage. This is a loan for a specified amount targeted for a specific purpose (such as a major home improvement project) that is repayable over a fixed period. It differs from a personal loan in that the property serves as security for the loan. The interest rate on such a loan is normally higher than for a first mortgage but less than for an unsecured (personal) loan.

Home equity loans

Another way to take advantage of the equity in a home is to take out a home equity loan. Because the debt is secured by the home, all or part of the interest is deductible, regardless of how the money is spent. As discussed previously, homeowners may either borrow a fixed amount that is repayable in equal monthly installments or establish a line of credit that allows them to borrow funds, as they are needed. An advantage of home equity loans is that the interest may be deductible. You as the borrower should be certain that you understand and will be able to meet the repayment terms. Because your house is the collateral for the loan, you risk losing your home in the event you are unable to repay the loan.

Refinancing

Interest rates are falling, and at the time of this writing, they can't fall much lower. You may be able to significantly reduce your monthly mortgage payment by refinancing your mortgage at a lower interest rate. By obtaining a mortgage that is greater than the outstanding balance of your existing mortgage, you also can cash in on your homeowner's equity ownership without selling the house. Even if the new loan is with the same lender, refinancing usually involves going through closing (and paying closing costs) all over again. A prepayment penalty on the mortgage could result in a significant additional expense, so check your mortgage documents before proceeding with refinancing. Shop around for the best terms, just as you did for your original mortgage - again comparing closing costs as well as the annual percentage rate.

WARNING

Be careful of the many refinancing companies that offer you amazing opportunities to get money out of your home. Many of these companies offer unethically high interest rates, hidden fees and prepayment penalties. I will cover refinancing in more detail in the upcoming the African American HomeBuyers Guide to Refinancing (2004) as well as on the website.

A saleable asset

You can turn your housing investment into cash by selling it. Because most people don't remain in the first home they buy for the rest of their lives, it is prudent to consider the resale value of a home from the outset, especially if you plan costly renovations.

Post-Purchase Checklist

Use this checklist to ensure that you are on the right track to successful homeownership:

_____ Move in.

_____ Organize a housewarming party! Meet the neighbors.

_____ Become familiar with the house.

_____ Establish a maintenance schedule and set aside funds for maintenance and routine repairs.

_____ Take safety precautions.

_____ Define the roles of people who live in the home.

_____ Set boundaries; make a list of house rules.

_____ Establish a household budget and take appropriate measures if you are overspending.

_____ Establish an emergency fund.

_____ Make your mortgage payments on time and get help immediately if you run into problems.

_____ Enjoy the tax and other financial benefits of homeownership!

Where we've been

We have been through the entire home buying and much of the homeowning process. You should be proud and confident that you are now a home buying expert. Go out buy a home. Help someone else buy a home. Maybe buy several homes and take responsibility for an entire neighborhood. The choices and opportunities are endless. African Americans are a glorious and victorious people and so are you. Contact me and the AAHBG family at AAHBG.com and let us know how much you enjoyed this book and what we can do to make it better. Take care of yourself, your people and your home.

Affirmation

I am the creator of my destiny. I have the power to determine my happiness, health and joy. Today, I am choosing victory.

Appendixes
Resources

Organizations That Help You Buy a Home

Fannie Mae
3900 Wisconsin Avenue, NW
Washington, DC 20016
1-800-732-6643
Web sites: www.fanniemae.com
Fannie Mae's Web sites provide in-depth information on many topics related to purchasing a home, including lists of lenders that offer mortgages.

Freddie Mac
401 9th Street, NW
Suite 600 South
Washington, DC 20004
(202) 434-8600
Web sites: www.freddiemac.com
Freddie Mac's Web sites provide in-depth information on many topics related to purchasing a home, including homes for sale and lenders that offer mortgages

Department of Housing and Urban Development (HUD)
Library and Information Services
HUD Building
451 Seventh Street, SW
Washington, DC 20410
Web site: www.hud.gov
HUD's homeownership opportunities and home improvement programs are available to individual households through state and local agencies or organizations. HUD also investigates housing-related discrimination complaints. Select from the following telephone numbers to obtain information about programs:

To reach HUD's Customer Service Center, call 1-800-733-4663.

To reach HUD's Housing Discrimination Hotline, call 1-800-669-9777.

For information on HUD programs, regional offices, and publications, call **(202) 708-1420.**

For Fair Housing information and materials, call **1-800-767-7468.**

ENFORCEMENT AUTHORITIES:

Federal Deposit Insurance Corporation (FDIC)
Compliance and Consumer Affairs Division
550 17th Street., NW
Washington, DC 20429
Toll free: 1-800-934-3342 FDIC handles questions about deposit insurance coverage and complaints about FDIC-insured state banks which are not members of the Federal Reserve System.

Office of Thrift Supervision (OTS)
Division of Consumer and Civil Rights
1700 G Street, NW
Washington, DC 20552
Toll free: 1-800-842-6929 OTS handles complaints about Federal savings and loans and Federal savings banks.

National Credit Union Administration (NCUA)
1175 Duke Street
Alexandria, VA 22314-3428
(703) 518-6330 The NCUA Shared Insurance Fund provides Federal insurance for nearly 13,000 credit unions.

Farm Credit Administration (FCA)
Director
Office of Congressional and Public Affairs
Farm Credit Administration
1501 Farm Credit Drive

McLean, VA 22102-5090 FCA regulates banks, associations, and related entities that comprise the Farm Credit System, including the Federal Agricultural Mortgage Corporation (Farmer Mac)

Comptroller of the Currency (OCC)
Compliance Management
250 E. Street, SW
Mail Stop 309
Washington, DC 20219
Toll free: 1-800-613-6743 OCC handles complaints and regulates National Banks. (Usually have "National" in name or "N.A." after their names.)

The Federal Reserve Board
Division of Consumer and Community Affairs
20th and C Streets, NW
Mail Stop 801
Washington, DC 20551
(202) 452-3693 Handles complaints and regulates state-chartered banks and trusts.
Administers Truth-in-Lending, Equal Credit Opportunity Act, and Fair Credit Reporting Act.

Housing Assistance Programs
This listing is for the each States Housing Agency
Call and ask for available housing assistance programs, including downpayment assistance

Alabama Housing Finance Authority
P.O. Box 230909 Montgomery, AL 36123-0909
(205) 242-4310

Alaska Housing Finance Corp.
P.O. Box 101020 235 East 8th Avenue
Anchorage, AK 99510
(907) 561-1900

Arizona Department of Commerce Office of Housing Development
1700 West Washington Phoenix, AZ 85007
(602) 280-1365

Arkansas Development Finance Authority
P.O. Box 8023 100 Main Street / Suite 200
Little Rock, AR
(501) 682-5900

California Housing Finance Agency
1121 L Street / 7th Floor Sacramento, CA 95815
(916) 322-3991

California Department of Housing & Community Development
P.O. Box 952050 Sacramento, CA 94252-2050
(916) 322-1560

Colorado Housing and Finance Authority
1981 Blake Street Denver, CO 80202
(303) 297-7427

Connecticut Housing Finance Authority
40 Cold Spring Road Rocky Hill, CT 06067
(203) 721-9501

**Delaware State Housing Authority
Division of** Housing and Community Development
18 the Green P.O. Box 1401 Dover, DE 19901
(302) 739-4263

DC Housing Finance Agency
1401 New York Avenue NW Suite 540
Washington, DC 20005
(202) 535-1353

Florida Housing Finance Agency
2571 Executive Center Circle East
Tallahassee, FL 32399
(904) 488-4197

Georgia Residential Finance Authority
60 Executive Parkway South / Suite 250
Atlanta, GA 30329
(404) 679-4840

Hawaii Housing Authority
1002 North School Street P.O. Box 17907
Honolulu, HI 96817
(808) 848-3277

Idaho Housing Agency
760 W. Myrtle Boise, ID 83702
(208) 336-0161

Illinois Housing Development Authority
401 N. Michigan Avenue / Suite 900
Chicago, IL 60611
(800) 942-8439 or
(312) 836-5200

Indiana Housing Finance Authority
One North Capitol / Suite 515 Indianapolis, IN 46204
(317) 232-7777

Iowa Finance Authority
100 East Grand Avenue / Suite 250 Des Moines, IA 50309
(515) 281-4058

Kansas Office of Housing Department of Commerce
400 S.W. 8th / 5th Floor Topeka, KS 66603
(913) 296-3481

Kentucky Housing Corporation
1231 Louisville Road Frankfort, KY 40601
(800) 633-8896
(502) 564-7630

Louisiana Housing Finance Agency
5615 Corporate / Suite 6A Baton Rouge, LA 70808-2515
(504) 925-3675

Maine State Housing Authority
P.O. Box 2669 295 Water Street Augusta, ME 04330
(800) 452-4668
(207) 626-4600

Maryland Department of Housing and Community Development
45 Calvert Street Annapolis, MD 21401
(301) 974-2176

Massachusetts Housing Financing Agency
50 Milk Street Boston, MA 02190
(617) 451-3480

Michigan State Housing Development Authority
Plaza One / Fourth Floor 401 South Washington Square P.O. Box 48909
(800) 327-9158
(517) 373-8370

Minnesota Housing Finance Agency
400 Sibley Street St. Paul, MN 55101
(800) 652-9747
(612) 296-9951

Mississippi Home Corporation
510 George Street / Suite 107 Dickson Building Jackson, MS 39201
(601) 359-6700

Missouri Housing Development Commission
3770 Broadway Kansas City, MO 64111
(816) 756-3790

Montana Board of Housing
2001 Eleventh Avenue Helena, MT 59620
(406) 444-3040

Nebraska Investment Finance Authority
1033 O Street / Suite 218 Lincoln, NE 68508
(402) 434-3900

Nevada Department of Commerce Housing Division
1802 N. Carson Street / Suite 154 Carson City, NV 89710
(702) 687-4258

New Hampshire Housing Finance Authority
P.O. Box 5087 Manchester, NH 03108
(603) 472-8623

New Jersey Housing Agency
3625 Quakerbridge Road Trenton, NJ 08650-2085
(800) NJ-HOUSE
(609) 890-1300

Mortgage Finance Authority
P.O. Box 2047 Albuquerque, NM 87103
(800) 444-6880
(505) 843-6880

State of New York Division of Housing and Community Renewal
One Fordham Plaza Bronx, NY 10458
(212) 519-5700

New York State Housing Authority
250 Broadway New York, NY 10007
(212) 306-3000

Appendix: Resources and Organizations   163

North Carolina Housing Finance Agency
3300 Drake Circle / Suite 200 Raleigh, NC 27611
(919) 781-6115

North Dakota Housing Finance Agency
P.O. Box 1535 Bismarck, ND 58502
(701) 224-3434

Ohio Housing Finance Agency
775 High Street / 26th Floor Columbus, OH 43266
(614) 466-7970

Oklahoma Housing Finance Agency
P.O. Box 26720 Oklahoma City, OK 73126-0720
(800) 256-1489
(405) 848-1144

Oregon Housing Agency Housing Division
1600 State Street / Suite 100 Salem, OR 97310
(503) 378-4343

Pennsylvania Housing Finance Agency
2101 North Front Street Harrisburg, PA 17105
(717) 780-3800

Rhode Island Housing and Mortgage Finance Corp.
60 Eddy Street Providence, RI 02903
(401) 751-5566

South Carolina State Housing Financing and Development Authority
1710 Gervais Street / Suite 300 Columbia, SC 29201
(803) 734-8836

South Dakota Housing Development Authority
P.O. Box 1237 Pierre, SD 57501
(605) 773-3181

Tennessee Housing Development Agency
700 Landmark Center 401 Church Street Nashville, TN 37219
(615) 741-4979

Texas Housing Agency
P.O. Box 13941 Capitol Station Austin, TX 78711
(512) 472-7500

Utah Housing Finance Agency
177 East 100 South Salt Lake City, UT 84111
(801) 521-6950

Vermont Housing Finance Agency
One Burlington Square
P.O. Box 408 Burlington, VT 05402
(800) 222-VFHA
(802) 864-5743

Vermont State Housing Authority
P.O. Box 397 Montpelier, VT 05601-0397
(802) 828-3295

Virginia Housing Development Authority
601 S. Belvedere Street Richmond, VA 23220
(804) 782-1986

Washington State Housing Finance Commission
111 Third Avenue / Suite 2240 Seattle, WA 98101-3202
(206) 464-7139

West Virginia Housing Development Fund
814 Virginia Street East Charleston, WV 25301
(304) 345-6475

Wisconsin Housing and Economic Development Authority
P.O. Box 1728 Madison, WI 53701
(800) 362-2767

Wyoming Community Development Authority
123 S. Durbin Street P.O. Box 634 Casper, WY 82602
(307) 265-0603

Downpayment Assistance

The follwing is a list of downpayment and home buying support agencies that help with financial gifts, grants or loans available to 1st time homebuyers. Go on the internet and type in Housing Assistance or Downpayment assistance and contact the appropriate agency. Many people do not even attempt to use these agencies for various reasons. You can afford to buy a home today with the help these agencies offer.

Nehemiah Program
www.nehemiahprogram.org
(800) 634-3642
This non-profit organization provides down payment gifts for FHA borrowers
The Nehemiah Program® has helped more than 151,000 families become home owners nationwide

This is a partial list of the Down Payment Assistance Programs (" DAPs "). I have not called all of these agencies, so I am not sure what service you will receive but do let me know. Viisit AAHBG.com and leave a comment so that I can update the website and future books.

PROGRAM NAME	DAP Maximum Assistance Amount	Contact	Phone #
16:15 Outfitters - Global Gift Charity The Global Gift Program (GIFT)	$20,000	J. Rick Metz	(505) 250-4706
A New Horizon Credit Counseling Services Inc A New Horizon Down Payment Assistance Program (GIFT)	$25,000	Ryan Ketola	(800) 556-1548
Affordable Housing Alliance Gift Program (GIFT)	Max 5%	Daniel Dotson	(425) 347-5353
Affordable Housing Concepts Inc The OWN Program (OP)	Max 5%	Rita McKenna	(727) 392-6676
AGAPE Economic Development Inc. AGAPE Down Payment Assistance Program (ADPAP)	Max 5%	Miguel Chavez	(562) 924-9655
Alpha Assistance Inc Down Payment Assistance Gift Program (GIFT)	$15,000	Michael Fisher	(770) 446-5496
American Assistance Corporation Home Ownership Gift Program (GIFT)	$10,000	Mark Walz	(972) 423-0394
American Assistance Foundation, Inc. - Gift Program (GIFT)	$10,000	Julie Donnelly	(703) 591-7107
AmeriDream Charity, Inc. Downpayment Gift Program (GIFT)	Max 5%	Ryan Hill	(301) 977-9133
Assistance Fund Down Payment Assistance Gift Program (GIFT)	$25,000	Gina Tyree	(877) 844-7419
Buckingham Foundation, Inc. Buckingham Foundation Home Buyers Assistance Program (GIFT)	$12,500	Aaron Hyman	(800) 531-2210
Buyers Dream Fund, Inc. Liberty Gold, Inc. The Down Payment Assistance Program (GIFT)	$18,000	Eli Tamkin	(216) 320-0870
Buyer's Fund, Inc. Neighborhood Gold GIFT Program	No Restrictions	David Hagen	(801) 636-2517
C-CAP Inc Gift Program (GIFT)	5.00%	Scott Fergus	(800) 590-1745
Chapel of Hope Ministries, Inc Homes of Hope Gift Program (HOH)	$40,000	Frank E Graham Jr	(972) 980-1009
Christ Centered Ministries, Inc. Gift Program (GIFT)	$25,000	David Forbes Morgan	(303) 832-7309
Community Housing and Development Corporation/ Responsible Home Ownership, Inc. Gift Program	No Restrictions	Stewart Vener	(800) 734-3633
Community Housing Assistance Program Inc CHAPA Homebuyer Gift Program	No Restriction	Kenneth Robertson	(714) 744-6252
Confederated Tribes of Siletz Indians Down Payment Grant (DPG)	$20,000	David Litchy	(503) 304-4064

PROGRAM NAME	DAP Maximum Assistance Amount	Contact	Phone #
Consumer Debt Solutions, Inc. HomeGrants Program (GIFT)	$25,000	Kimberly Carlson	(845) 691-9697
Cornerstone Ministries Down Payment Assistance Program (DAP)	Max 3%	Clare Weakley, Jr.	(800) 614-1144
Creativity Innovation Productivity Inc DBA Horizon Event Foundation - Homebuyer Grant Program (GRANT)	$15,000	Ed Kanavel	(801) 601-3131
CREED-The Center of Resources for Economic Education and Development Inc. American Dream Gift Program (GIFT)	$25,000	David Diaz	(915) 682-2520
Crumbs Charity Corporation Down Payment Assistance Gift Program (GIFT)	$25,000	Larry James Johnson	(410) 426-5026
Deep South Community Development Corporation Down Payment Assistance Gift Program (GIFT)	$17,200	Johnny Fogle	(404) 241-4060
Defeat Diabetes Foundation IncRealMONEY Grant Program (GIFT)	Max 10%	Gerald Mandell	(727) 139-5050
Del Sol Foundation Down Payment Gift Program (GIFT)	$25,000	Noemi Beas	(562) 622-5322
Dove Foundation, Inc American Family Funds Down Payment Gift Program (GIFT)	No Restrictions	Marc Whitehead	(251) 344-1084
Down Payment Fund Gift Program (GIFT)	No Restrictions	Brian Haveman	(800) 620-2239
DPA Alliance Corporation Gift Program (GIFT)	$20,000	Pam Ogden	(801) 687-0538
DreamHome Foundation Down Payment Grant Program (GRANT)	25000	Mike Rath	(888) 801-6400
Dreamhouse Charity Inc Gift Program (GIFT)	$100,000	Jason Wilson	(503) 582-0706
Employer Assisted Housing Program (refer to WF guidelines)	$50,000	N/A	(000) 000-0000
Esther Foundation, Inc. Down Payment Assistance Grant (GRANT)	$50,000	Eric Scott	(866) 937-8437
Family Home Provider Inc Program (FFHP)	Max 6%	Fred Proctor	(770) 887-4578
Family Housing Foundation Affordable Housing Gift Program (Gift)	$25,000	Bob Garrett	(806) 356-4080
Foundation For Housing Assistance Grant Program (FFHA)	No Restrictions	Dennis O'Rourke	(216) 521-4663
Foundation For Life Enhancement, Inc. HomeBuyers Financial Program Foundation For Life Enhancement Grant Program (GIFT)	$40,000	James Hadsell	(800) 493-5156
Franklin Foundation Inc. Key Grant Program (GIFT)	$15,000	Scott Nash	(301) 869-2900
Futures Home Assistance Program (Gift)	Max 6%	Ed Hays	(800) 672-4055
Genesis Foundation, Inc.The Preferred Downpayment Assistance Program (GIFT)	$40,000	Keith Heckler	(866) 570-0830
Genesis Housing Development Corp. Genesis Program	$22,500	S. Kevin Smith	(512) 231-0270
GiftAmerican Program, Inc. Down Payment Gift Program (GIFT)	$25,000	Michelle Hurney	(301) 231-0028
God is King Foundation Gift Program (GIK)	$15,000	Derrick Fenner	(206) 715-3238
Harford Food Bank Inc Downpayment Grant Program (GIFT)	Max 10%	Rev. Ric McNally	(410) 272-1883
Home Buyers Assistance Foundation Gift Program	Max 7.5%	Rebecca Wallace	(770) 471-6890
Home Downpayment Gift Foundation Inc Charitable Gift Program (GIFT)	$25,000	Rick Delsantro	(888) 856-4600
Home Gift USA Charities, Inc. Gift Program (GIFT)	$25,000	Gary Cain	(407) 841-6855

PROGRAM NAME	DAP Maximum Assistance Amount	Contact	Phone #
Home Ownership Foundation Inc Buyer's Hope Down Payment Gift Program (GIFT)	$35,000	Tom Whitley	(888) 240-7283
Home Ownership Providers Inc Zero Down Payment Affordable Housing Program (ZDP)	Max 3%	Marlene Wade	(770) 509-2234
Homebuyers Assistance Fund, Inc. - Homebuyers Assistance Program	$25,000	Brad L Smith	(866) 211-0740
Homeownership Foundation of America Inc/New Life Family Housing Group Inc Gift Program (GIFT)	Max 9%	Shawn Beatty	(410) 285-8711
Homes For All, Inc. Downpayment Gift Program	Max 7%	Robert Shellman	(941) 656-4255
Horizon Community Finance Fund Inc. Down Payment Assistance Gift Program (GIFT)	$35,000	Mel Weger	(800) 348-8888
Housing Action Resource Trust (HART) Down Payment Assistant Program (DPA)	$15,000	Melissa Simmons	(909) 945-1574
Housing Corporation of America GIFT Program (GIFT)	Max 6%	Steve Sanders	(801) 328-3644
Individual Freedom Ministries Church Gift Program (GIFT)	$25,000	Perry Traylor	(904) 789-8451
International Housing Solutions, Inc. Colorado Care DreamMaker, and NAREB Programs (GIFT)	25,000	Stacy Crandall	(800) 894-1444
Jeremiah Foundation, Inc. Jeremiah Down Payment Assistance Program (JDAP)	$25,000	Jeffrey L. Greene	(866) 823-7653
Jewish Vocational Service and Community Workshop JVS Downpayment Assistance Program (GIFT)	$40,000	Jay Penfil	(248) 559-5000
Ken-Ray Inc Down Payment Assistance Program (DPAP)	No Restrictions	Curtis Turnbull	(801) 225-0750
Keystone Grants Inc/NovusAmerica LLC The Keystone Plan (GIFT)	$40,000	Mark Gurley	(888) 785-7526
Main Street Foundation, Inc. Down Payment Assistance Program (GIFT)	$30,000	Wrennie Stewart	(866) 678-1977
Mid-America Teen Challenge Training Center, Inc. Mid-West Housing Authority Grant Program (GRANT)	$35,000	Robert Baltzell	(866) 239-1515
Multi State Equity Funding Corporation Affordable Home Ownership Program (AHOP)	$10,000	Sharon Albright	(515) 327-1911
Multi State Federal Home Loan Bank of Topeka Rural First-time Homebuyer Program (RFHP)	$4,000	Michele Carter	(866) 571-8155
Multi State Federal Home Loan Bank of Topeka Targeted Ownership Program (TOP)	4,000	Linda Cooper	(408) 776-7284
Multi State Shuttlesworth Housing Foundation Program (GIFT)	$2,000		(513) 721-6855
Multi State World Missions Equity Grants Down Payment Gift Fund Program (GIFT)	5% MAX	Dan Hibma	(616) 257-5250
National Home Charities, Inc. – Down Payment Assistance Program (GIFT)	$31,000	Dale Goodnight	(303) 410-9893
National Home Foundation – Downpayment Gift Program (GIFT)	$25,000	David Diaz	(915) 682-2520
National Home/JW Hansen Community Foundation Gift Program (GIFT)	$24,000	Jeffrey W. Hansen	(916) 685-5797
Nehemiah Corporation The Nehemiah Program®	Max 6 %	Hiedi	(916) 231-0350
Neighborhood Housing Services, HomeStart Downpayment Assistance Gift (DPAG)	$10,000	Laura Cruz	(909) 884-6891
New Age Home Ownership Assistance Foundation New Age Assistance Program Gift (NAAP)	Max 5%	Patrick Hataburde	(708) 239-5978
New Home Gallery, Inc. Gift Program (GIFT)	$25,000	Judy Parr	(502) 412-9163

PROGRAM NAME	DAP Maximum Assistance Amount	Contact	Phone #
Newsong Fund Down Payment Assistance (DPA)	Max 20%	Steve Dyer	(888) 901-5715
North American Housing Foundation – NOAH Gift Program (GIFT)	$25,000	Lloyd Herman	(509) 961-6346
Officer Next Door (refer to WF guidelines)	$120,000		(202) 708-1672
Partners in Charity, Inc. (PIC) Gift Program	Max 10%	George Yates	(800) 705-8350
Prairie Band Potawatomi Nation Down Payment Gift Program (GIFT)	$10,000	Jack Kitchdommie	(866) 966-2756
Southlake Harbor Baptist Church Harbor Trust Program (GIFT)	Max 3%	Matthew Turner	(817) 416-5459
Su Casita Inc Gift Program (GIFT)	$25,000	Cliff Oswalt	(512) 478-2900
Sustainable Living Foundation – Down Payment Gift Program (GIFT)	$25,000	David Diaz	(915) 682-2520
Sweet Home Foundation Gift Program (GIFT)	$8,000	Lisa Kinsey	(208) 454-0014
Teacher Next Door (refer to WF guidelines)	$120,000		(202) 708-1672
United American Housing and Education Foundation (UAHEF), Alliance Housing Assistance Program - Gift Program	$10,000	David Hail	(972) 722-1927
Westminster Foundation Inc HomeStart Program (GIFT)	3% MAX	Everett Terry	(404) 758-0021
Zebra Project Inc. Gift Program (GIFT)	Max 8%	John Fuller	(404) 759-4800

How Much Money Is It – Finder

Use the following tables to determine your **approximate** monthly mortgage payment (principal and interest) when you already know the loan amount. If you want to know how you can afford to spend each month find the amount in the table and you can determine the interest rate and the mortgage associated with that amount.

Loan Amount	Interest Rate								
	5.0%	5.5%	6.0%	6.5%	7.0%	7.5%	8.0%	8.5%	9.0%
$50,000	$269	$284	$300	$317	$333	$350	$367	$385	$403
$60,000	$322	$341	$360	$380	$400	$420	$440	$461	$483
$70,000	$376	$398	$420	$443	$466	$490	$514	$538	$564
$80,000	$430	$454	$480	$506	$533	$560	$587	$615	$644
$90,000	$483	$511	$540	$570	$599	$630	$661	$692	$725
$100,000	$537	$568	$600	$633	$666	$700	$734	$769	$805
$110,000	$591	$625	$660	$696	$733	$770	$807	$846	$886
$120,000	$644	$682	$720	$760	$799	$840	$881	$923	$966
$130,000	$698	$738	$780	$823	$866	$910	$954	$1,000	$1,047
$140,000	$752	$795	$840	$886	$932	$980	$1,028	$1,077	$1,127
$150,000	$806	$852	$900	$950	$999	$1,050	$1,101	$1,154	$1,208
$160,000	$859	$909	$960	$1,013	$1,066	$1,120	$1,174	$1,230	$1,288
$170,000	$913	$966	$1,020	$1,076	$1,132	$1,190	$1,248	$1,307	$1,369
$180,000	$967	$1,022	$1,080	$1,139	$1,199	$1,260	$1,321	$1,384	$1,449
$190,000	$1,020	$1,079	$1,140	$1,203	$1,265	$1,330	$1,395	$1,461	$1,530
$200,000	$1,074	$1,136	$1,200	$1,266	$1,332	$1,400	$1,468	$1,538	$1,610
$210,000	$1,128	$1,193	$1,260	$1,329	$1,399	$1,470	$1,541	$1,615	$1,691
$220,000	$1,181	$1,250	$1,320	$1,393	$1,465	$1,540	$1,615	$1,692	$1,771
$230,000	$1,235	$1,306	$1,380	$1,456	$1,532	$1,610	$1,688	$1,769	$1,852
$240,000	$1,289	$1,363	$1,440	$1,519	$1,598	$1,680	$1,762	$1,846	$1,932
$250,000	$1,343	$1,420	$1,500	$1,583	$1,665	$1,750	$1,835	$1,923	$2,013
$300,000	$1,611	$1,704	$1,800	$1,899	$1,998	$2,100	$2,202	$2,307	$2,415
$350,000	$1,880	$1,988	$2,100	$2,216	$2,331	$2,450	$2,569	$2,692	$2,818
$400,000	$2,148	$2,272	$2,400	$2,532	$2,664	$2,800	$2,936	$3,076	$3,220
$450,000	$2,417	$2,556	$2,700	$2,849	$2,997	$3,150	$3,303	$3,461	$3,623
$500,000	$2,685	$2,840	$3,000	$3,165	$3,330	$3,500	$3,670	$3,845	$4,025

How Much Money Is It – Finder (continued)

Use the following tables to determine your **approximate** monthly mortgage payment (principal and interest) when you already know the loan amount. If you want to know how you can afford to spend each month find the amount in the table and you can determine the interest rate and the mortgage associated with that amount.

Loan Amount	Interest Rate								
	9.5%	10.0%	10.5%	11.0%	11.5%	12.0%	12.5%	13.0%	13.5%
$50,000	$421	$439	$458	$477	$496	$515	$534	$554	$573
$60,000	$505	$527	$549	$572	$595	$617	$641	$664	$688
$70,000	$589	$615	$641	$667	$694	$720	$748	$775	$802
$80,000	$673	$702	$732	$762	$793	$823	$854	$886	$917
$90,000	$757	$790	$824	$858	$892	$926	$961	$996	$1,031
$100,000	$841	$878	$915	$953	$991	$1,029	$1,068	$1,107	$1,146
$110,000	$925	$966	$1,007	$1,048	$1,090	$1,132	$1,175	$1,218	$1,261
$120,000	$1,009	$1,054	$1,098	$1,144	$1,189	$1,235	$1,282	$1,328	$1,375
$130,000	$1,093	$1,141	$1,190	$1,239	$1,288	$1,338	$1,388	$1,439	$1,490
$140,000	$1,177	$1,229	$1,281	$1,334	$1,387	$1,441	$1,495	$1,550	$1,604
$150,000	$1,262	$1,317	$1,373	$1,430	$1,487	$1,544	$1,602	$1,661	$1,719
$160,000	$1,346	$1,405	$1,464	$1,525	$1,586	$1,646	$1,709	$1,771	$1,834
$170,000	$1,430	$1,493	$1,556	$1,620	$1,685	$1,749	$1,816	$1,882	$1,948
$180,000	$1,514	$1,580	$1,647	$1,715	$1,784	$1,852	$1,922	$1,993	$2,063
$190,000	$1,598	$1,668	$1,739	$1,811	$1,883	$1,955	$2,029	$2,103	$2,177
$200,000	$1,682	$1,756	$1,830	$1,906	$1,982	$2,058	$2,136	$2,214	$2,292
$210,000	$1,766	$1,844	$1,922	$2,001	$2,081	$2,161	$2,243	$2,325	$2,407
$220,000	$1,850	$1,932	$2,013	$2,097	$2,180	$2,264	$2,350	$2,435	$2,521
$230,000	$1,934	$2,019	$2,105	$2,192	$2,279	$2,367	$2,456	$2,546	$2,636
$240,000	$2,018	$2,107	$2,196	$2,287	$2,378	$2,470	$2,563	$2,657	$2,750
$250,000	$2,103	$2,195	$2,288	$2,383	$2,478	$2,573	$2,670	$2,768	$2,865
$300,000	$2,523	$2,634	$2,745	$2,859	$2,973	$3,087	$3,204	$3,321	$3,438
$350,000	$2,944	$3,073	$3,203	$3,336	$3,469	$3,602	$3,738	$3,875	$4,011
$400,000	$3,364	$3,512	$3,660	$3,812	$3,964	$4,116	$4,272	$4,428	$4,584
$450,000	$3,785	$3,951	$4,118	$4,289	$4,460	$4,631	$4,806	$4,982	$5,157
$500,000	$4,205	$4,390	$4,575	$4,765	$4,955	$5,145	$5,340	$5,535	$5,730

Pre-Application Information Worksheet

To be used to complete loan applications

Page 1 of 2

Borrower's Name _____

Social Security # _____

Current Address _____

Home phone ( ) _____ **Work phone** ( ) _____

Co-Borrower's Name _____

Social Security # _____

Current Address _____

Home phone ( ) _____ **Work phone** ( ) _____

Address of Purchase Property _____

Price of Property $ _____ **Mortgage Amount** $ _____

Type of Loan Term   ☐ 30 years   ☐ 15 years   ☐ 1 year

Employment (past three years) start with current employer for all borrowers

Employer Name	Work Address & Telephone #	Start and End Date	Current or Final Salary
_____	_____	_____	_____
_____	_____	_____	_____
_____	_____	_____	_____

Landlord (past three years) start with most recent address for all borrowers

Landlord Name	Your Previous Addresses	Mo/Year Rented	Monthly Rent $
_____	_____	_____	_____
_____	_____	_____	_____
_____	_____	_____	_____

Appendix: Pre-Application Information Worksheet

Pre-Application Information Worksheet (continued)

To be used to complete loan applications

Page 2 of 2

Bank Accounts – checking, savings, etc.

Bank Name	Address & Telephone #	Account Number	Monthly Payment	Current Balance

Credit Cards – bank, department stores, etc.

Name of Creditor	Address & Telephone #	Account Number	Monthly Payment	Current Balance

Loan information – car loan, student loan, etc.

Name of Lender	Address & Telephone #	Account Number	Monthly Payment	Current Balance

Remember to bring the following with you:

- [ ] Personal check for loan application fee
- [ ] Purchase and sale agreement
- [ ] Copy of real estate listing of house you are buying
- [ ] Photocopy of earnest money check

Each borrower on the loan application should bring:

- [ ] Payroll stub from employer, W-2 forms for past two years, or other proof of employment and salary (if self-employed: balance sheets, tax returns for the past two years, and year-to-date profit and loss statement)
- [ ] Photocopies of last three monthly bank statements for all checking and savings accounts
- [ ] Company name, number, and value of stocks and bonds you own
- [ ] Make, year, and value of all automobiles you own
- [ ] Information on real estate you already own
- [ ] If establishing a nontraditional credit history: canceled checks or money order receipts as evidence of rental, utility, or other payments
- [ ] Evidence of any non-employment income (disability benefits, trust income, etc.)

Budget Worksheet

MONTHLY BUDGET to help you track your monthly income and expenses

INCOME		HOUSING EXPENSES	
Monthly Salary (after taxes)	$	Rent/Mortgage	$
Monthly Salary (2nd job)	$	Property tax/ insurance	$
Net Overtime pay	$	Home maintenance	$
Pension, Social Security benefits	$	Electricity	$
Investment earnings	$	Gas/Oil	$
Public assistance	$	Water	$
Alimony/child support	$	Other	$
Other income	$	**NON-HOUSING EXPENSES**	
		Food	$
TOTAL MONTHLY INCOME	$	Clothing	$
TOTAL MONTHLY EXPENSES	$	Day care/tuition	$
INCOME AFTER EXPENSES (Income minus Expenses)	$	Car loans(s)	$
		Car insurance/tax	$
		Gas and oil	$
		Car repairs	$
		Bus/Train (Transportation)	$
		Health care	$
		Credit card #1	$
		Credit card #2	$
		Other loan payments	$
		Alimony/child support	$
		Entertainment	$
		Telephone	$
		Cable	$
		Insurance (other than car)	$
		Savings	$
		Other	
		TOTAL MONTHLY EXPENSES	$

Mortgage Shopping Comparison Worksheet

Type of Loan: _____ _____ (Fixed or adjustable) _____

Term: _____ _____ Number of Years of Loan _____

Lock Period: _____ _____ Days (30, 45, 60 days) _____

Loan Amount: _____ _____

Interest Rate: _____ _____ (APR the total cost of loan) _____

Fee _____ Percent of Loan _____ Dollars _____

Payable to Borrower or the Lender _____ _____

Application Fee* _____ Flat fee paid normally paid upfront _____

Commitment Fee* _____ Flat fee _____

Points _____ Based on % of loan _____

Origination Fee _____

Mortgage Broker Fee _____ Based on % of loan _____

All Other Fees _____ _____

Payable to Third Parties _____ _____

Credit Report Fee _____ _____

Appraisal Fee _____ _____

Other Fees _____ _____

Total _____ _____

*Paid before closing. If credited against other fees, deduct from the other fees.

Name of mortgage broker: _____

Signature: _____

Top Ten Black Cities For Living and Working*

Modified from the list published by Black Enterprise

		FINAL TALLY			
TOP 10 CITIES	B.E. RANKING	FINAL SCORE	TOTAL POPULATION	BLACK POPULATION	BLACK %
Houston, TX	1	70.58	1,953,631	494,496	25.3
Washington, D.C.	2	69.45	572,059	343,312	60.0
Atlanta, GA	3	68.99	416,474	255,689	61.4
Charlotte, NC	4	65.18	540,828	176,964	32.7
Memphis, TN	5	63.79	650,100	399,208	61.4
Detroit, MI	6	62.37	951,270	775,772	81.6
Baltimore, MD	7	61.99	651,154	418,951	64.3
Dallas, TX	8	61.18	1,188,580	307,957	25.9
Chicago, IL	9	60.22	2,896,016	1,065,009	36.8
Philadelphia, PA	10	59.54	1,517,550	655,824	43.2
National Average	N/A	N/A	281,421,906*	34,658,190*	12.3
B.E. Top 10 Average	N/A	64.33	1,133,766	489,318	49.26

* For the purposes of this story, "cities" are U.S. Census Bureau-defined Urbanized Areas, which consist of a central city of at least 50,000 residents, and a population density of at least 1,000 people per square mile of land area.

Top Ten Black Cities for African American Homeowners

TOP 10 CITIES	COST OF LIVING INDEX**	AVG. HOUSE PRICE**	AVG. RENT**	BLACK MORTGAGE REJECTION %**	BLACK/WHITE REJECTION RATIO**
Houston, TX	93.1	$108,500	$610	40.57	1.61:1
Washington, D.C.	124.0	176,400	830	24.77	3.01:1
Atlanta, GA	103.2	126,800	590	30.63	1.95:1
Charlotte, NC	100.1	139,400	560	N/A	N/A
Memphis, TN	92.4	114,600	540	36.18	2.17:1
Detroit, MI	105.2	140,600	640	36.21	1.52:1
Baltimore, MD	97.0	126,800	640	28.89	2.73:1
Dallas, TX	100.5	126,000	730	40.71	1.64:1
Chicago, IL	111.3	170,200	750	32.68	3.93:1
Philadelphia, PA	100.0	128,572	N/A	28.64	3:20:1
National Average	100.0	128,572	N/A	53.75	1.96:1

Glossary

Acre
A measurement for property. One acre equals 43,560 square feet. The median lot size for the United States is one-third of an acre.

Acceleration clause
A clause in a mortgage stating that the entire loan balance shall become due immediately if a breach of certain conditions occurs.

Adjustable-rate mortgage (ARM)
A mortgage that permits the lender to adjust the interest rate periodically on the basis of changes in a specified index.

Amortization
The gradual repayment of a mortgage by installments, calculated to pay off the obligation at the end of a fixed period of time.

Annual percentage rate (APR)
The total cost of a mortgage stated as a yearly rate; includes the base interest rate, loan origination fee (points), commitment fees, prepaid interest, and credit costs that may be paid by the borrower.

Appraisal
A professional estimate of the market value of a property, based on prices that have been recently paid for similar properties in the same area.

Appreciation
An increase in the value of a property due to changes in market conditions or other causes.

APR
See annual percentage rate.

ARM
See adjustable-rate mortgage.

Asbestos
Once a common form of insulation for hot-water pipes. Frequently removed by specialists if frayed, but left in place if properly sealed.

Assessed value
The valuation placed upon property that is used to compute property taxes.

Assets
How a banker measures the value of your possessions, such as money or cars, and commitments due to you, such as salary or alimony. Assets are offset by liabilities to determine your net worth.

Assumable mortgage
A mortgage that can be taken over by the buyer when a home is sold.

Assumption fee
A processing fee paid to the lender upon the transfer of the seller's existing mortgage to the buyer.

Automated underwriting
A tool (such as Fannie Mae's Desktop Underwriter and Desktop Home Counselor) that automates the process of qualifying and underwriting borrowers.

Bid
The offer of how much you're willing to pay for a house.

Binder
A preliminary agreement between a homebuyer and seller that includes the price and terms of the contract.

Blockbusting
The illegal practice of inducing panic selling in a neighborhood by making representations of the entry, or prospective entry, of members of a minority group (from internet)

Cap
A provision of an ARM limiting how much the interest rate or mortgage payments may increase.

Capital gains tax
A tax levied on profits realized from the sale of capital assets, including houses and other real property.

Cash reserves
A requirement that buyers have sufficient cash remaining after closing (such as two months' mortgage payments).

Clear title
A title that is free of liens or legal questions as to ownership of property.

Closing
A meeting to finalize the sale of property by delivery of a deed from seller to buyer. The buyer signs the mortgage documents and pays the closing costs. Also called "settlement."

Closing costs
The upfront expenses that must be paid at the time of purchase (over and above the price of the property). Some of these expenses are typically paid by the buyer and others by the seller.

Combined loan-to-value (CLTV) ratio
The ratio between the total amount of mortgages (including any subordinate financing) and the appraised value of the property.

Commission
A fee, usually a percentage of the purchase price of the property, paid to a real estate agent.

Commitment letter
A formal offer by a lender stating the terms under which it agrees to lend money to a homebuyer.

Community Home Buyer's Program
A Fannie Mae mortgage targeting low- and middle-income borrowers that allows a low down payment and no cash reserves at closing.

Community Lending
A group of flexible Fannie Mae loan products designed to expand the availability of mortgages for low- and moderate-income families.

Condominium (condo)
A form of shared ownership of a property, typically used in apartments and town houses. A condo owner owns his unit but shares ownership (and upkeep cost) of the roof, cellar, entrance walks, and other common areas.

Community Seconds loan
A subsidized second mortgage or ("soft second") that is issued by a housing agency or nonprofit organization. Payment is usually deferred or forgiven over time and carries no or low interest rates.

Condominium
A form of property ownership in which the owner holds title to an individual dwelling unit, while the facilities and common areas are owned collectively by the owners of a multi-unit project.

Conservator
An individual or organization that has been named by a court to exercise control over a person (or in some states, a person's estate).

Contingency
A condition that must be met before a contract is legally binding.

Contract
A legal agreement between you and the seller to transfer ownership in a house for a set price.

Conventional mortgage
Any mortgage that is not insured or guaranteed by the federal government.

Convertible ARM
An adjustable-rate mortgage that may be converted to a fixed-rate mortgage under specified conditions.

Cooperative
A type of ownership in which the residents of a multiunit housing complex own shares in a corporation, giving each resident the right to occupy a specific unit.

Counteroffer
Response from a seller to a buyer's offer. A counteroffer is typically higher than the buyer's offer and lower than the original sales price of the house.

Covenant
A clause in a mortgage that obligates or restricts the borrower and which, if violated, can result in foreclosure.

Credit counselor
A person who is trained to give advice about money management. The counselor may work for a lender, mortgage insurer, or independent credit counseling agency.

Credit report
A report of an individual's credit history prepared by a credit bureau and used by a lender in determining a loan applicant's creditworthiness.

Credit scoring
A process by which credit bureaus summarize a borrower's credit history in the form of a score that many lenders use to evaluate a loan applicant's creditworthiness.

Deductible
A set amount that an insured person pays out of his or her own funds to cover repairs or replacement of lost or damaged property.

Deed
A legal document conveying title to a property.

Deed of trust
A document used in some states in place of a mortgage that gives the lender a security interest in the property. Title is conveyed to a trustee who holds title to the property until the loan is paid off.

Default
The failure to make a mortgage payment on a timely basis or to comply with other requirements of a mortgage.

Deficiency judgment
A judgment for the balance of the debt following the foreclosure of a mortgage.

Delinquency
A situation in which a payment on a loan is overdue but not yet in default.

Deposit
A "good faith" payment submitted by a buyer along with a purchase offer; the payment is held in escrow and is returned if the seller doesn't accept the buyer's offer. Also called "earnest money."

Down payment
The portion of the purchase price that the buyer pays in cash and does not finance with a mortgage.

Early delinquency counseling
A requirement of certain Fannie Mae loan products in which mortgage servicers refer borrowers who fail to make a mortgage payment on time to a third-party counseling agency to help resolve any problems.

Earnest money
A deposit submitted by a buyer along with an offer to purchase a house.

Easement
A right of way giving persons other than the owner access to or over property.

Equal Credit Opportunity Act
A federal law passed in 1974 that prohibits lenders from discriminating on the basis of a borrower's race, sex, religion, age, national origin, receipt of public assistance funds, marital status, or disability.

Equity
A homeowner's financial interest in a property. Equity is the difference between the market value of the property and the amount still owed on the mortgage.

Escrow
The holding of the buyer's deposit by the real estate agent prior to closing; also, an account into which a portion of the mortgage payment is held by the lender for payment of taxes and insurance on the borrower's behalf.

Exclusive listing
An agency's monopoly right to sell a house for a period of time. If another agent brings in the seller, the exclusive agency still receives a portion of the sale.

Fair Credit Reporting Act
A federal law that guarantees individuals the right to examine the information about them on file with a credit report agency.

Fannie 97
A Fannie Mae mortgage for low- and moderate-income homebuyers that requires only a 3 percent down payment and allows higher-than-normal qualifying ratios.

FHA mortgage
A mortgage that is insured by the Federal Housing Administration, a unit of the U.S. Department of Housing and Urban Development (HUD).

First mortgage
A mortgage that has first claim to the secured property in the event of default.

Fixed-rate mortgage
A mortgage in which the interest rate does not change during the entire term of the loan.

Flood insurance
Insurance that compensates for property damage resulting from flooding.

Forbearance
The lender's postponement of foreclosure to give the borrower time to catch up on overdue payments.

Foreclosure
Legal action taken by a lender if a borrower fails to pay monthly mortgage payments on time. The lender takes back the property and sells it to try to recover the money loaned.

FSBO
"For sale by owner" is when an individual sells his home without a broker.

Grace period
The length of time after the payment due date that a lender or other creditor will allow a monthly payment to be paid without charging a penalty.

Graduated payment mortgage
A mortgage that starts with low monthly payments that increases at a predetermined rate for a specified time.

Grant
Money that does not need to be repaid; grants to homebuyers may be available from government agencies, including affordable housing programs, or private foundations and nonprofits.

Guardian
An individual or organization who has been named by a court to exercise some or all powers and rights over a person or a person's estate.

Hazard insurance
Insurance coverage that compensates for damage to a property from fire, wind, vandalism, or other hazards.

Home inspection
A property inspection to evaluate the structural and mechanical condition (but not the market value) of a property based on observable, unconcealed structural conditions.

Homebuyer education
A requirement of some Fannie Mae loan products in which borrowers take a series of classes designed to ensure that they are prepared for the responsibilities of homeownership.

HomeChoice loan
A Fannie Mae mortgage targeting low- and moderate-income homebuyers with disabilities (or who have family members with disabilities living with them). These loans allow very low down payments and higher-than-normal qualifying ratios.

Homeowner's insurance
An insurance policy that combines personal liability coverage and hazard insurance coverage for a dwelling and its contents.

Homeowner's warranty
An insurance policy that covers repairs to a home's major systems (such as the heating system, air conditioning, and major appliances), usually in the first year following purchase.

Housing counselor/education provider
A person who is trained to provide pre-purchase homebuyer education and otherwise assist prospective homebuyers throughout the purchase process.

Housing finance agency
A state-mandated agency that provides financing for low- and moderate-income homebuyers.

HUD
U.S. Department of Housing and Urban Development.

HUD-1 Settlement Statement
A federally mandated form used to itemize charges to the buyer and the seller.

Interest
The fee charged for borrowing money.

Interest rate cap
A provision of an ARM limiting how much the interest rate may increase per adjustment period or over the life of a mortgage.

Joint tenancy
A form of co-ownership giving each owner equal interest and rights in the property, including the right of survivorship.

Late charge
A penalty imposed by the lender when a payment is received after the due date.

Lease-Purchase Mortgage Loan
A Fannie Mae mortgage product under which the homebuyer leases a home from a nonprofit organization or private seller with an option to buy. Each month's rent payment includes an amount that accumulates toward the down payment.

Liabilities
Any obligations, such as a credit-card balance or student loan, which you must pay on a regular basis.

Lien
A legal claim against a property that must be paid off when the property is sold.

Lifetime cap
A provision of an ARM that limits the total increase in the interest rate over the life of the loan.

Loan interview
A meeting between the person applying for a mortgage and the loan officer.

Loan officer
An agent of the lending institution who collects the information that the loan underwriter uses to evaluate the loan application.

Loan origination fee
A charge imposed by the lender to cover the administrative costs of processing the loan.

Loan processing
The steps performed by the lender to determine whether to grant or deny a loan.

Loan servicing
The collection of mortgage payments from borrowers and the related responsibilities of a loan servicer.

Loan term
The number of years over which the mortgage is to be repaid.

Loan-to-value (LTV) ratio
The relationship between the unpaid principal balance of the loan and the appraised value of the property.

Lock-in
An agreement guaranteeing the borrower a specified interest rate provided the loan is closed within a set period of time.

Market value
The final sale price of a house – as opposed to assessed value.

Medicaid
A federal/state program that provides medical services to low-income people, including people with disabilities.

Mortgage
A legal document that pledges a property to the lender as security for repayment of a loan.

Mortgage broker
An individual or company that, for a fee, acts as intermediary between borrowers and lenders.

Mortgage insurance (MI)
Insurance paid for by the borrower that protects the lender against loss if the buyer fails to repay the mortgage loan.

Mortgage life insurance
A type of insurance that automatically pays off the mortgage in the event of the borrower's death.

Mortgage margin
The set percentage the lender adds to the index value to determine the interest rate of an ARM.

Mortgage note
A legal document obligating the borrower to repay a loan at a stated interest rate during a specified period of time. The mortgage note is secured by a mortgage.

Mortgagee
The lender in a mortgage agreement.

Mortgagor
The borrower in a mortgage agreement.

Multiple listing service (MLS)
A computerized system that generates a list of properties for sale. A way for real estate agents to share houses they are selling (or listing) with agents from other firms that may be representing buyers.

Negative amortization
A gradual increase in the mortgage debt that occurs when the monthly payment is not large enough to cover the entire amount of principal and interest due.

Nontraditional credit history
Documentation of a borrower's monthly rent, utility, and other payments that do not appear on a traditional credit report; canceled checks, receipts, and letters from creditors may be used to supplement a traditional credit report (but not to "fix" a derogatory credit history).

Occupancy date
The date that a buyer may move into a newly purchased home.

Open house
Listed in the newspaper, these houses are for sale and are open for certain hours for anyone to visit without an appointment.

Origination fee
A fee paid to the lender for processing a loan application.

Owner financing
A transaction in which the property seller provides all or part of the financing.

Panic Peddling
The illegal practice of inducing panic selling in a neighborhood by making representations of the entry, or prospective entry, of members of a minority group.

Payment cap
A provision of some ARMs limiting the amount of a borrower's payments, regardless of the interest rate increase; may result in negative amortization.

PITI
An abbreviation that stands for principal, interest, taxes, and insurance - the components of a monthly mortgage payment.

Planned unit development (PUD)
A development plan for a tract of land that provides for residential and commercial uses and for supporting services such as schools and recreational facilities.

Points
A one-time fee charged by the lender to originate the mortgage; a point is 1 percent of the amount of the mortgage.

Prepaids
Fees collected from the buyer at closing to cover items such as property taxes and homeowner's insurance that the seller has already paid.

Prepayment penalty
A fee that may be charged by a lender if the borrower pays off a loan before it is due.

Prequalification
The process of determining how much money prospective home buyers will be eligible to borrow in advance of applying for a mortgage.

Principal
The amount borrowed or remaining unpaid; also, the portion of the monthly mortgage payment that reduces the outstanding balance.

Probate court
A court that has jurisdiction over wills and may oversee guardianships and conservatorships.

Property inspection
An inspection to evaluate the structural and mechanical condition of a property based on observable, unconcealed structural conditions.

Purchase and sale agreement
A written contract signed by the buyer and seller stating the terms and conditions under which a property will be sold.

Qualifying ratios
The ratios that are used to compare the buyer's monthly housing costs (PITI) and total debt (including housing costs) with the buyer's monthly gross income. These ratios are used to determine how large a loan to grant a homebuyer.

Rate lock-in
An agreement guaranteeing the homebuyer a specified interest rate provided the loan is closed within a set period of time.

Real Estate Settlement Procedures Act (RESPA)
A consumer protection law that requires lenders to give borrowers advance notice of closing costs.

Real Estate Taxes
Local government assessments to pay for schools, sewers, and other municipal amenities.

Realtor
A trademark of the National Association of Realtors. Although many people use the term generically, not all real estate agents are Realtors.

Recording fee
A fee charged for the filing of a legal instrument in a county's public records.

Redlining
The illegal practice of refusing to originate mortgage loans, or limiting their number, in certain neighborhoods on the basis of racial or ethnic composition.

Refinancing
The process of paying off one loan with the proceeds from a new loan using the same property as security.

Representative payee
A person or organization selected by the Social Security Administration to manage the benefit payments of individuals receiving Supplemental Security Income (SSI) or Social Security Disability Insurance (SSDI).

Reserves
A requirement of many mortgages that buyers have sufficient cash remaining after closing to cover one or two months' mortgage payments.

Restrictive Covenant
An agreement by property owners in a neighborhood not to sell or rent their property to African Americans or minorities for a definite period

Rider
An addendum to an insurance policy that provides specific additional coverage.

Rural Housing Service (RHS) mortgages
Low-interest, no-down-payment mortgages offered to low- and moderate-income homebuyers in rural areas by RHS, a branch of the U.S. Department of Agriculture.

Second mortgage
A mortgage that has a lien position subordinate to the first mortgage.

Servicing
A lender's responsibilities that include collecting and accounting for mortgage payments, handling escrow funds, following up on delinquencies, and remitting and reporting to investors.

Settlement agent
A lender, title insurance company, escrow company, real estate broker, or attorney who conducts the loan closing.

Social Security Disability Insurance (SSDI)
A Social Security benefit available to disabled workers based on time employed and past earnings.

Steering
The illegal practice of directing members of minority groups to, or away from, certain areas, or neighborhoods.

Supplemental Security Income (SSI)
A Social Security benefit available to disabled persons with limited income and resources.

Survey
A drawing or map that shows the precise legal boundaries of a property and

physical features, such as improvements to the property (buildings, fences, etc.).

Sweat equity
The value you put into your home by doing improvements yourself rather than hiring outside labor.

Tenancy by entirety
A type of joint ownership that provides rights of survivorship and is available only to a husband and wife.

Tenancy in common
A type of joint ownership in a property without rights of survivorship.

Title
A legal document evidencing property ownership.

Title Company
A company that specializes in examining and insuring titles to real estate.

Title insurance
Insurance to protect the lender (lender's policy) or the buyer (owner's policy) against loss arising from disputes over ownership of a property.

Title search
An examination of the public records to ensure the seller is the legal owner of the property and to determine whether there are any liens or other claims outstanding.

Transfer of servicing
The transfer of responsibility for servicing a mortgage (collecting and processing the borrower's monthly payments) from one lender to another.

Transfer tax
A state or local tax payable upon the transfer of real property.

Trust
A legal agreement in which one person places money or property in the name of an individual or organization (the trustee) to be used for the benefit of another person (the beneficiary).

Truth-in-Lending Act (TILA) Act
A federal law that requires lenders to fully disclose, in writing, the terms, and conditions of a mortgage, including the APR and other charges.

Underwriting
The process of evaluating a loan application to determine the risk involved for the lender. It involves an analysis of the borrower's creditworthiness and the value of the property.

VA mortgage
A loan that is guaranteed by the Veterans Administration and allows qualified veterans to buy a house with no down payment.

Walk-through
A buyer's final inspection of the house being bought prior to loan closing.

Zoning laws
Local laws that control what can be built on a particular piece of property. Zoning laws generally keep commercial and residential districts separate.

Index

1

10 Credit Scams That Affect African Americans, 67–70

A

Adjustable-rate mortgages, 108
Adjustment interval., 111
Advantages Of Homeownership, 17
Affidavits, 132
Affirmation, 15, 28, 52, 79, 100, 122, 134, 159
African Proverb, 3
Afryka, Imani, 3
Ali, Muhammad, 12
Allowable monthly housing expense, 62
Alternatives to foreclosure, 145
America's Homeownership Challenge, 9
American Dream Commitment, 9
American Dream Downpayment Fund, 9
American Society of Home Inspectors, 98
Analyzing your credit, 63
and Freddie Mac, 39
Annual percentage rate, 109
Answer Sheet
  Questions to ask Mortgage Broker. *See* Mortgage Broker
Application options., 109
Appraisal contingency, 96
Appraiser, 35
Approval of mortgage insurer, 118
ARM terms, 141
ARMs, 108
Asbestos, 99
, 58
Assets, 58
Assets For Downpayment Worksheet, 58
Assumability., 110
Atlanta Housing Authority. *See* Stewart, Janice
attitude, 8, 11
Automated underwriting, 116
automatic payment, 127

Avoiding Foreclosure, 143

B

Bethune, Mary McLeod, 135
Bird, Larry Bird. *See* Home Dream Team
Biweekly payment schedule, 141
Black Enterprise, 10
Black Folks Guide to Making Big Money in America, 11
borrowing power, 76
Bowie, Maryland, 19
Broker, 46, 47, 48
Bush, George, 9
Buyer's Remorse, 133

C

Cancellation of mortgage insurance, 143
Capacity, 57, 114
Capital, 57, 115
Capital gains exclusion, 157
Carver Federal, 9
cash reserves, 126
Chatham, Chicago, Illinois, 19
Children of Homeowners, 18
Civil Rights Act, 8, 121
Closing cost
  final estimate, 129
Closing costs., 56
Closing costs/fees., 109
closing date, 124
Closing Day, 130
Coalition for Responsible Lending, 121
Collateral, 57, 115
Commercial Banks, 36
Commitment letter, 118
Commitments To Becoming A Homeowner, 8
Community Property, 23
Community Status, 18
Community-based organizations, 78
Comparison shopping, 91
Complaint of Incorrect Credit Info, 82
Comptroller of the Currency, 162
Condominium, 25

Contacting the servicer, 144
Contingencies, 96
Contractor, 36
Conventional loans, 103
Convertibility., 111
Cooperative, 26
Co-Owners, 21
Costs Of Purchasing A House, 55, 80
Creating a budget, 151
Credit Card Accounts, 65
credit counselor, 145
Credit Form Letters, 80
Credit history, 57, 115
Credit History, 63
Credit report
    free request, 81
Credit Report Factors, 63
Credit Scams, 67
Credit scoring, 116
Credit Scoring, 64
Credit Unions, 38

D

Debt, 72
deed, 131
Deed in lieu of foreclosure, 146
Deed of trust, 132
Department of Housing and Urban
    Development, 8
Depreciation of rental income, 156
Determining total monthly expenses,
    152
Determining total net income, 152
dishonest "buyers", 146
documentation, 113
Down payment, 55
Down payment requirement., 109

E

Earnest money, 97
Ebony, 10
Eliminating Credit Card Debt, 72
Ellington, Duke, 135
Emergency Numbers, 138
Energy conservation, 147
Enforcement authorities, 161
Equifax, 32, 66
Equity investment, 19
Erroneous Credit Record, 66
Escrow accounts, 132
Escrow adjustments, 142
Escrow agent, 38

Escrow requirement., 110
Essence, 10
Evers-Williams, Myrlie, 29
Experian, 32, 66
Extra payments, 141

F

Fair Housing Act, 8, 91, 120
Fair, Isaacs and Company. *See* FICO
Fannie Lou Hamer, 8
Fannie Mae, 9, 10, 17, 39, 70, 71, 77,
    102, 103, 105, 106, 107, 109, 112,
    116, 117, 145, 146, 150, 154, 161,
    177, 179, 180, 181
Farm Credit Administration, 161
Federal Deposit Insurance Corporation,
    161
Federal Housing Administration, 104
, 26
Federal Reserve Board, 162
fees for Condo/co-op, 57
FICO, 32
Filing cabinet, 31
final purchase price, 97
Financial and Real Estate Industry's
    Commitment, 9
Financial Incentives, 19
Financial index., 111
Financing major repairs, 150
Financing terms, 96
Finding a lender, 102
Fire Safety, 138
Fixed-rate mortgages, 108
Flood Insurance, 139
Forbearance, 146
Foreclosure, 89, 143, 180. *See*

, 82
Formaldehyde, 99
Four C's\ of underwriting, 114

G

Garvey, Marcus, 29
Gates Jr., Henry Louis, 87
Gifts., 77
Giovanni, Nikki, 123
government assistance, 20
Government-insured loans, 104
Grants., 77
Greater Harlem Real Estate Board, 10
Guides to Success, 15

Index   **187**

H

Harlem Renaissance, 19
Hazardous waste sites, 99
Home
   Searching for, 88
Home Dream Team, 31, 34
Home equity loans, 151, 157
Home improvement and personal loans, 150
Home improvements, 149
Home Inspection, 98
Home-buying checklist, 100
Home-in-a-Box, 30, 34, 52, 74, 137, 139, 157
homeowner's equity, 157
homeowner's insurance, 125
homeowner's warranty, 127
Homeownership readiness checklist, 78
House search
   Construction details, 92
   Major systems, 93
   Physical details, 92
Household budgeting, 151
housing finance agencies, 78
Housing Finance Agency, 50
how much to offer, 94
HUD, 8, 9, 20, 26, 77, 91, 104, 107, 129, 145, 157, 161, 179, 181
Hurston, Zora Neale, 101

I

Ikeda, Daisaku, 14
Impact of Homeownership on Child Outcomes, 18
Improving your ratios
   ratios, 63
Initial interest rate., 111
Insufficient funds, 119
Insufficient income, 119
Insurance Agent, 39, 40
Insurance coverage, 139
Interest deduction, 156
Interest rate., 108

J

Johnson, Magic. *See* Home Dream Team
Joint Center for Housing Studies, Harvard, 18
Joint Tenancy, 22
Jordan, Michael. *See* Home Dream Team

K

Keeping Your Current Job, 73
King, Dr. Martin Luther, 8

L

Late Payment, 83
Lead-based paint inspection, 97, 59
Lending Discrimination, 121
Living within one's budget, 155
loan application, 112
Loan assumption, 146
Loan interview, 113
Loan modification, 146
Loan Officer, 41
Loan processing, 114
Loan Qualifications
   Understanding, 57
Loan Servicer, 41
Loan types, 103
Loanology, 107, 108
Loans. *See* Mortgages

M

Maintenance
   Expenses, 57
Manufactured Homes, 26
Margin., 111
Market value, 94
McCarthy, Osceola, 53
Medicaid, 20, 127, 155, 182
Mitchelville, Maryland, 19
Mobile Home, 26
Monthly mortgage payment, 56
mortgage, 131
Mortgage Banker, 42
Mortgage Broker, 43, 45
Mortgage checklist, 122
Mortgage insurance, 109
Mortgage Life Insurance, 140
Mortgages, 108
Mozilo, Angelo R., 5
Multi-family homes, 26

N

NAACP, 10
Nam myoho renge kyo, 74
National Credit Union Administration, 161
Negotiating The Home Purchase, 93

Neighbors, 137
nontraditional credit history, 70
note, 131

O

of Explanation of Employment Gap, 76
Office of Thrift Supervision, 161
Olympic Dream Team. *See* Home Dream Team
Ongoing costs. *See* Cost of Purchasing a House
On-Time, 75
Orlando Rivera, 10
Owner financing, 93

P

Partnerships, 23
Payment cap., 111
Payment options., 110
Payment Terms, 140
Personal Touch, The: What you Really Need to Succeed in Today's Fast-Paced Business World, 75
Points., 108
Post-Purchase Checklist, 159
Pre-Application Information Worksheet, 171
Pre-approval, 54
Pre-Closing Checklist, 133
Pre-foreclosure sale, 146
Prepayment Fee, 110
Pre-qualification, 54
President's Commitment, 9
Preventive maintenance, 147
Private Mortgage Insurance, 109
Processing time., 109
Property appraisal, 115
property survey, 126
Property tax deduction, 156
Property/Mechanical Inspector, 46
Public Benefits, 76
Purchasing title insurance, 124

Q

qualifying ratios. *See* Lender qualifications

R

Racism, 11, 12

Radon inspection, 97
Raines, Franklin D., 17
Randolph, A. Phillip, 8
Rate caps., 111
Rate lock-in., 110
Real Estate Agent, 46, 48
Real Estate Attorney, 48
Reasons of Credit Denial, 85
Refinancing, 158
Repairing a Bad Credit Record, 66
Repairs
    expenses, 57
Repayment plan, 146
Repayment term., 109
Reporting suspected discrimination, 120
Responsibilities of Homeownership, 20
Robeson, Paul, 123
Rural Housing Service, 104

S

Safety tips, 137
saleable asset, selling your home, 158
sales agreement, 95
Satisfactory home inspection, 96
Savings & Loans, 36
Second mortgages, 157
Section 8, 9, 20
Seller, 38, 50, 103
Servicing issues, 142
Servicing problems, 143
Setting financial goals, 155
Settlement Agreement, 84
Settling-in costs, 56
Sharing the Cost of Homeownership, 21
Sherman, William T., 7
Shopping for a mortgage, 102
Single Owner, 21
Single-Family Affordable Housing Tax Credit, 9
Single-family home, 25
Sources of mortgages, 102
Sources of supplemental financing, 77
Stability, 18
Stable housing costs, 19
state certification, 127
Stewart, Janice, 4
Strengthening Black Communities, 18
Subsidized second loans., 77
Success-ism, 11
Supplemental Financing, 77
Supplemental Security Income, 20
Support Person, 51, 52

Index 189

T

Tax benefits, 19, 156
Taxes and insurance, 57
Tenants-in-common, 23
Termite and other inspections, 96
termite certificate, 126
The Black Church, 10
Theft Prevention, 138
title search, 124
Title VIII, 8, 121
Top Ten Black Cities, 175
Townhouse, 25
Trans Union, 32, 66
Transfer of servicing, 142
Trower-Subira, George, 11
Truth-in-Lending Act, 130

U

Upfront costs. *See* Cost of Purchasing a House
Urban League, National, 10

Utilities, 57

V

Variety of Homes
 Home Variety, 25
Veterans Administration, 104

W

Walker, Mme C.J., 87
walk-through. *See* Closing Day
Washington, Booker T., 101
Water inspection, 97
Williams, Serena, 13
Williams, Terrie, 75
Williams, Venus, 13
Wilson, Gloria, 21
Winfrey, Oprah, 7
Woods, Tiger, 13
Woodson, Carter G., 53
Working Skills, 75

BIBLIOGRAPHY

The research and data that went into this guide was derived from a tremendous amount of resources, interviews and conferences. I am providing the primary sources (that I could locate) for which I am deeply indebted and grateful.

FannieMae (www.fanniemae.com)
FannieMae Foundation (www.fanniemaefoudation.com)
Various reports and studies and the major source of information for this guide is from their website.

Responsiblelending.org
Various reports on predatory lending; presentation made at Citigroup's annual stockholders meeting, 2003 New York, NY.

Jt. Center for Housing Studies, Harvard
The Social Benefits and Costs of Homeownership:
A Critical Assessment of the Research, W. Rohe, S. Van Zandt and G. McCarthy October 2001
The Industrial Structure of Affordable Mortgage Lending, F. Nothaft and B Surette, July 2001
The Anatomy of the Low-Income Homeownership Boom in the 1990s, M. Duda and E. Belsky, July 2001
The Impact of Homeowenrship on Child Outcomes, D. Haurin, T. Parcel and R Haurin, October 2001
The State of the Nations Housing Report, 2002

US Department of Commerce
Black in America 1992
Census Reports: Various datasets
The Department of Housing and Development
American Housing Survey for the United States: 2001

Office of Thrift Supervision
Eighth Annual Economic Development Summit, Remarks by Ellen Seidman, Director, March 14, 2001

Black Enterprise
Various issues: Including annual BE Top 100

The University Georgia, Georgia Minority Economic Power Report
The Multicultural Economy 2002
Minority buying power in the new century
Jeffrey M. Humphreys

Acorn Report
Predatory Lending 2001

Department of Housing and Urban Development (HUD)
Homeownership and Affordable Housing: The Opportunities
(February 1990, 41 p.)

Living With Racism: The Black Middle-Class Experience, J. Feagin and M. Sikes, Beacon Press 1994

Black Folks Guide to Making Big Money in America, George Subira, Published by Very Serious Business Enterprises: Contact your local bookstore and order.

The Personal Touch: What You Really Need to Succeed in Today's Fast-Paced Business World., Terrie Williams, 1994, Warner Books -- includes a foreword by Bill Cosby and a preface by Jonathan M. Tisch, the president and CEO of Loews Hotels

Interviews and conversations of hundreds of Homebuyers and Homeowners from many beautiful and various ethnicities and cultures. Thank you all.